£7.99

65

4

8

KT-568-827

# Just
# start

LEONARD A. SCHLESINGER

CHARLES F. KIEFER

with **PAUL B. BROWN**

# *Just* start

Take **action,** embrace **uncertainty,** create **the future**

Harvard Business Review Press

*Boston, Massachusetts*

Copyright 2012 Harvard Business School Publishing Corporation
All rights reserved

Printed in the United States of America
10 9 8 7 6 5 4 3 2 1

Library of Congress Cataloging-in-Publication Data

Schlesinger, Leonard A.
    Take action, embrace uncertainty, and create the future / Leonard A. Schlesinger and
Charles F. Kiefer with Paul B. Brown.
        p. cm.
    ISBN 978-1-4221-4361-2 (alk. paper)
    1. Success in business.    2. Creative ability in business.    3.    Problem solving.    I.
Kiefer, Charles F.    II.  Brown, Paul B.    III.  Title.
    HF5386.S386 2012
    658.4'09—dc23

                                                                        2011040328

*To Saras D. Sarasvathy,*
*whose research and insights remind us*
*how we can all think and act entrepreneurially.*

A journey of a thousand miles begins with a single step.

—Lao-tzu, Chinese philosopher (604 BC–531 BC)

So, start!

—Leonard A. Schlesinger, Charles F. Kiefer, and Paul B. Brown

Our promise to you:

If you employ the handful of principles in the following pages, whatever you want will come closer within reach.

Postscript: You will notice we are not guaranteeing success. But we are guaranteeing that if you fail, you will fail quickly and cheaply, and that (as you will see) is almost as good.

# Contents

*Introduction*
# Navigating Uncertainty

Our intellectual journey—as teachers, innovators and business-people—was to answer the question of how can you achieve success in an uncertain world. To find out, we looked to those who thrive best in uncertain environments: serial entrepreneurs. When we did, we learned they not only think differently, but act differently, too. Based on their experience, we constructed a step-by-step proven method to navigate through uncertain environments. We've distilled the very essence of what makes people successful in uncertainty and show how it works for everyone, everywhere. This process has worked for us. We know it will work for you as well and, as a very pleasant byproduct, we truly believe it will make the world a slightly better place.

ARE YOU FRUSTRATED? We know we are.

Most of us prepared hard for the future we expected, and yet the future isn't working out as we had planned. That's true if you have been laid off, are a recent college graduate who feels underemployed, a manager facing constant upheavals at work, or even if you are the boss, because you are wrestling with disruptive technologies and new competitors who seemingly come out of nowhere to upend your industry. All this is extremely confusing and unsettling.

This is *not* how we were told it was going to be. Growing up, we were led to believe that the future was predictable, and if we studied hard, we could obtain the work we wanted in an environment we understood, and we would live happy and successful lives.

It hasn't exactly turned out that way (even for those of us who are happy). Many of us, maybe most, are not making progress on achieving what we want.

We think the reason is pretty simple. The way we were taught to think and act works well in a predictable future, but not so much in the world as it is now.

You know the steps for dealing with a predictable universe:

1. You (or your parents, teachers, or bosses) forecast how the future will be.

2. You construct a number of plans for achieving that future, picking the optimal one.

3. You amass all the resources (education, money, etc.) necessary to achieve your plan.

4. And then you go out and make that plan a reality.

Our education and our organizations have so indoctrinated us in this way of thinking that it is more or less the only way we approach anything. But what is a very smart approach in a knowable or predictable future is not smart at all when things can't be predicted, and that fact is at the heart of the frustrations most of us feel. Things simply aren't as predictable as they once were.

In a world where you can no longer plan or predict your way to success, what is the best way to achieve your goals? It's a daunting question, but today—when saying "change seems to be the only constant" has become a cliché because it is true—it's one everyone has to resolve.

We think this book provides an answer. It starts with the premise that the world is probably going to get more unpredictable than less, so the ways of thinking that have gotten us where we are will be even more insufficient going forward. What follows from that is that we need a new way of thinking, one that complements, not replaces, the way we were taught to reason. (Much will remain predictable and you don't want to abandon a set of skills that works well in certain situations. You just want to have new tools for new situations.) You will find that new way of acting in the pages ahead.

Specifically, we are going to give you a proven method for dealing with uncertainty, a method gleaned from studying serial entrepreneurs—people who have started two or more successful companies. Why them? That's simple. They have mastered a process for dealing with the unknown. There is nothing more uncertain than starting at a company. Drawing on the way they approach and solve problems, we will show you:

- The best strategy and tactics to employ when the future is uncertain.

- How to minimize risk and cost in every decision you make.

- The best way to attract like-minded people to what you want to do. And

- Why "Act, Learn, Build, so you can Act again" is the best and most important course of action when facing the unknown.

These proven ideas work whether you are starting a new project at the office or starting your own company. In fact, they will be helpful in every part of your life. They will let you navigate uncertainty and help you achieve what you want.

## The Babson Connection

Reading one book can never be a substitute for a college education, but after you have finished this one, you'll have pretty good insight into how one of our leading schools thinks (and teaches) about business.

For as long as there have been national and worldwide rankings, Babson College has ranked first in teaching "entrepreneurship of all kinds."

If you look at the college's Web site you will see that right under its mission statement ("Babson College educates leaders who create great economic and social value—everywhere") is the explanation of the strategy that allows that to happen.

The first sentence is: "Babson College will be known as the preeminent institution for Entrepreneurial Thought and Action." Entrepreneurial Thought and Action is the school's (and our) shorthand way of describing much of the process in this book. The Babson faculty is committed to extending its research and teaching this method far beyond the introduction this book provides.

We know this approach works, because we used it ourselves in creating this book. It is also the approach that is used by the university—Babson College, the world's number-one school for entrepreneurship—of which one of us is president.

As we told our friends just before publication, a funny thing happened on the way to creating this book: we followed our own advice and ended up with something far different (and we think far better) than what we set out to do. Specifically, we discovered a method that has already improved our lives—and we believe can improve yours as well.

If we give you the back story to how this book came about, you'll be able to see how.

## We set off to do . . .

This was supposed to be a traditional business book. We planned to write fifty thousand or so words pointing out that entrepreneurs think differently from the rest of us. Not better, just differently. From there, we were going to say that their different way of thinking works particularly well when you can't predict the future with any real accuracy.

The logical conclusion from those first two findings was clear. Since we are facing a business environment that seems to grow more unpredictable every day (when we were working on this book in 2011, financial problems in Greece—Greece! the twenty-seventh largest economy in the world—threatened to take down the global financial markets), perhaps it was a good time to add the entrepreneurial lens to the way we view all business problems.

We weren't going to call for a wholesale revolution, like from now on you should *only* think like an entrepreneur; we were just going to suggest that you may want to add that entrepreneurial lens to your decision-making tool kit.

To be honest, we felt pretty good about what we were going to do. That book (like this one) would have been research based. We had a catchy title: *Thinking Upside Down*; a couple of major publishers were extremely interested in what we had to say, and we had even started to plan the clever bons mots we were going to drop when we were interviewed. So life was good and we started merrily on our way to creating *Thinking Upside Down* . . . and then the whole thing blew up in our faces.

## Oops!

We know exactly the moment everything changed. We had finished the chapter that explains the difference between the way most of us think and the way successful serial entrepreneurs (people who, as we said, have started multiple successful companies) reason. And, as we mentioned, the difference is particularly stark.

Starting well before we enter school, we were all taught what can best be described as prediction reasoning. *It is a pattern of thinking and acting based on the assumption that the future is going to behave in a way similar to the present and the immediate past.* It involves inferring and extrapolating, often using (sometimes very complex) analytic methods.

When we use prediction reasoning (we refer to it here as Prediction) in business, we begin with a predetermined goal: we want to create a new widget or a unique service. Then with the goal clearly established, we set off to identify the optimal, fastest, cheapest, most efficient way to accomplish the objective. This means identifying the necessary resources—the money, people, time, and so on—and planning how to best employ them. Deciding on make versus buy in production, choosing the target with the highest potential return in marketing, or picking a portfolio with the lowest risk in finance are all examples of Prediction.

---

Treating an uncertain world as if it were predictable only
gets you into trouble.

---

Most entrepreneurs, as we said, go about things differently. Sure, they use Prediction some of the time, especially when their firms are up and running and they are dealing with the business problems every other executive faces. But they also employ what we call *Creaction*, a word we made up by combining *creation* with *action*. Creaction boils down to this: the future may or may not be like the past, but you don't have to spend a lot of time wondering how it will play out if you plan to shape (i.e., create) it.

We were proud of that initial chapter, but when we finished it, we realized two things:

1. Yes, our central insight that serial entrepreneurs reason differently from the rest of us was intriguing, but the world was not waiting to read yet another "think differently" book. There have been 8,617 of them as far as we can tell (and Apple has been telling the world to "think different" since it made the phrase the basis of its advertising slogan in 1997).

2. Thinking (differently or otherwise) is great, but absolutely nothing changes unless you *act*. Painters can think all they want about painting, but until they pick up a brush, there is no picture. And if you are in business, you can think all you want about a new product or service, but until you act on the idea, there is nothing tangible to show for all that thought.

And that's when the proverbial penny dropped.

Yes, of course, entrepreneurs think differently. But equally importantly, their natural inclination is to put that thinking into immediate action to see if they are right.

The clichéd image of entrepreneurs coming up with an idea, laboring feverishly to perfect it, and delivering their creation to the market fully formed is not what usually happens, as you will see in chapter 5. The much more typical path is that they come up with an idea. They take a small step toward implementation to see if anyone is interested, and if it looks like there is potential market acceptance, they take another step forward. If they don't get the reaction they want, they regroup and then take another step in a different direction.

In other words, they

Act.

Learn (from that action), and

Build (off that learning), and act again.

That cycle repeats until the entrepreneur succeeds; knows she is not going to succeed, or decides there is another, more appealing opportunity to pursue.

The cycle of acting/learning/building/and-acting again to learn some more is what makes the way entrepreneurs think so different—and the way they think so important to the rest of us.

Traditionally, when we encounter an obstacle, we are told, "Don't be a wimp. You had a good plan. Redouble your efforts and power on through." That is classic Prediction. Since Prediction is about setting a goal and establishing an efficient or optimal plan based on a prediction about the future, once the goal is set, you are supposed to constantly correct to stay on plan. (Since the goal and plan are born from your prediction, they must be right.) Hence, when something goes awry, you *should* try harder.

Entrepreneurs take a different approach. They have an idea ("I want start my own business; I think I will start a public relations firm"), and they get underway.

Once they do, they judge the market's reaction. ("Gee, no one seems to be overly excited about yet another PR firm. But the few clients I have love the way I explain how they should communicate with their employees about what they are trying to do with their PR strategy. Maybe, I should forget about PR, which is about external communication, and concentrate on internal communication.")

In other words, entrepreneurs are not committed to the plan (starting a PR firm); they are committed to the goal (in this case, "starting a business of my own that would be fun and successful").

That is pure Creaction. Whereas in Prediction, anything that disrupts your plan or blows you off course—surprises, obstacles, and so on—is a negative, Creaction treats encountering these very same things as positives. ("The fact that no one wants another PR firm is a good thing; it shows me I shouldn't waste my time trying to build one; and it pointed me to the opportunity to do internal communications instead.")

When faced with an unknown future—"I wonder if anyone will hire my new PR firm"—entrepreneurs act to find out, instead of sitting there trying to predict what might happen. Their approach to dealing with an unknown future was the reason we decided to change our plans about what we were going to write.

---

If you can't predict the future—and increasingly you can't—
action trumps everything.

---

## When the light bulb went on

What we realized, as we took a step back, is not only that most entrepreneurs view the unforeseeable world differently, but how they go about tackling problems successfully can be chronicled and explained. In other words, *their methods are available to everyone.*

Until now, most studies of entrepreneurs have tended to focus on entrepreneurial behavior, which is indeed idiosyncratic; no two entrepreneurs do things exactly the same way. But we shouldn't have been looking only at their behavior. We should have been studying the thinking that leads to their behavior as well.

That was a huge "aha" moment for two reasons.

First, in a world that is seemingly growing more unpredictable by the moment, you can neither think of everything—or even close to everything—nor map out the future with any real certainty. That means that Prediction reasoning alone is incomplete today and may well become even more limiting tomorrow. Instead of *thinking* your way into a new way of acting, which is at the heart of using Prediction, you need *to act* your way into creating the future you want. That's what entrepreneurs do when faced with the unknowable—and it is an approach that will work for you as well.

Second, we came to understand that what entrepreneurs do will work everywhere!

A quick example will prove the point. Say you want to lose thirty pounds. You can think all you want about losing the weight, but if you keep your eating habits and exercise patterns exactly as they are, your weight will remain exactly where it is. Until you take action, nothing is going to change.

But what kind of action?

Well, in the Prediction world, you would work out a plan. Maybe you would stop eating carbohydrates, or follow the current hot diet. You'd keep your eye on the prize—losing those thirty pounds. And history shows that you will probably fail. The level of commitment required (high) and time frame (long) are just too much for most of us.

Someone who employs Creaction would attack the problem differently. They'd begin by taking what we have come to think of as a "smart step" (action) in the direction they want to go. It would not necessarily be overly aggressive ("I am only going to eat five hundred calories a day") or focus on a big goal ("I am going to lose those thirty pounds in the next sixty days").

That smart step probably would be a statement like: "I want to lose one pound this week."

With that modest initial goal in mind, you are far more likely to eat a little bit less over the next seven days and exercise a touch more. If at the end of the week, you have found that you have indeed lost a pound (or perhaps more), you will say to yourself, "That wasn't so bad. Let's see if I can do it again next week." And if you fail, you'd try adding something else. ("Hmmm. If I keep exercising and eating less and have just one glass of wine with dinner instead of two, maybe that will work.")

And if that approach is successful, you've learned something from *your own experience*, not just the diet book. So you build off your success and try it again the following week—and keep repeating it until you have achieved your goal. You have broken down a big problem ("How the heck am I ever going to lose thirty pounds?") into a series of smart actions: losing a pound a week for thirty weeks.

## Eureka!

You can see why we were so excited and wanted to share what we had discovered. In writing the original chapter, we had inadvertently employed Creaction, the creation reasoning used by successful entrepreneurs. We didn't plan it or do a market study of our potential audience. Instead, we invested just a little bit of time and effort and wrote a chapter; it didn't feel right ("do we really want to write another 'think differently' book?"). We learned something ("since creating that book doesn't excite us, let's figure out what does"), and we tried something else.

We scrapped our initial plan and turned the (negative) surprise we encountered (the world doesn't want a think differently book) into a positive—the book you are now reading.

While our focus is going to be employing Creaction in business (including starting new businesses) because we know these areas best, we will periodically sprinkle in other examples just to underscore that the concept of Entrepreneurial Thought and Action—the Babson faculty's term for using Prediction and Creation together—works everywhere.

Because this approach works everywhere, this is a book for everyone. We all are struggling with how to deal with a world that seems to grow more uncertain every day.

Until now, when faced with this problem, most of us have reacted in one of two ways, neither of them helpful. Either we freeze in place because we just don't know what to do or we have continued thinking that we can simply predict every bit of the future, uncertainty or no.

We are offering a third option. We want to make Entrepreneurial Thought and Action an inclusive and inviting concept that stimulates large-scale adoption of its methods by as many people as possible. That is how we can stimulate enormous economic and social value and build a world in which we can be much more optimistic.

Entrepreneurs have proven that this approach works. We have proven it for ourselves, and we are interested in hearing how it works for you. Please write to us at JustStartTheBook.com.

*Part One*

# What to Do When Facing the Unknown

# 1

# What to Do When You Can't Predict the Future

You may have wondered why so many things seem to be harder and take longer to accomplish than you would like— and why both those things seem to be increasing.

We don't have the answer in every case, but here is an explanation that probably covers the majority of situations: the way we have been taught to solve problems was designed for a different world. To deal with uncertainty today, we need a different approach.

YOU'RE SMART, creative, and terrific at approaching challenges. So why does it seem that the number of things you can't figure out is increasing? The problem may not be you. It could be the way you were taught to think. From kindergarten on, we've all learned prediction reasoning—a way of thinking based on the assumption that the future is going to be pretty much like the past.

Demographics are one simple example of how prediction reasoning (what we refer to as Prediction) works. You can calculate, with a some confidence, the world population in 2050 because you know a lot of things. Here are just four:

1.  You know how many people are alive today: about 7 billion.

2.  You know how those people are distributed by age, that is, you know how many teenagers there are, how many people over age sixty-five, and so on.

3.  That means you know how many people are in their twenties and thirties, when most people decide to have children.

4.  And you know recent trends in population growth, which is slowing as people worldwide are, on the whole, deciding to have fewer kids.

Studying all this data and much, much more, you can, as the United Nations did recently, say with reasonable certainty that in the year 2050, there will be 8.9 billion people on the planet. Armed with that data, you can also make a number of fairly accurate estimates, such as how many diapers will have to be produced, how many gallons of water those 8.9 billion people will drink each day, and how much the United States will need to pay out in Social Security benefits at the midpoint of this century.

We have gotten really good at Prediction. To support this kind of thinking, we have developed great analytic tools (statistics, probability theory, computer simulations, and the like). These tools are logically sound and complete. That's a scientist's way of saying they yield the correct solutions, and the same solutions, every time. Math like this is great. It has right and wrong answers, and is consistent. It allows us to do wondrous things. You want to send a rocket to the moon and land at a specific spot (even though the orbiting moon will be moving while the rocket is underway)? No problem. Prediction allows you to do that. Need to come up with a fairly precise estimate of how many sports cars will be sold during a recession? Prediction can help with that as well.

Because it works so well in these kinds of situations—and countless others—we (like you) became accustomed to using Prediction all the time. And like anything, if you do something over and over, it becomes a habit. Your view of the world becomes conditioned.

And yet... Not everything can be foreseen (and therefore predicted). Want to know if the cute guy across the hall is going to ask you out? Sorry, Prediction can't help. Desperately need to know if the town council is going to accept your idea of turning Main Street into a pedestrian mall, before you spend your nights and weekends working on the project? Prediction is of little use. Is the world ready for your brand-new, never-before-seen product or service? That's another place where Prediction really does you no good.

Here's the central point of this book: when the future is unknowable (Is quitting your job and starting something new a good idea? Will the prototype we are developing at work find a market?) how we traditionally reason is extremely limited in predicting what will happen.

You need a different approach.

We are going to give you a *proven* method for navigating in an uncertain world, an approach that will complement the kind of reasoning we have all been taught. It will help you deal with high levels of uncertainty, no matter what kind of situation you face. We know it works because entrepreneurs—the people who have to deal with uncertainty every day—use it successfully all the time.

## If it works for them . . .

When people write about entrepreneurs, they invariably focus on their behavior: what Howard Schultz or Michael Dell did in building their companies. If you take that approach, you probably would conclude that every single entrepreneur is unique, so there is little to be learned from studying them; you would have to be Howard Schultz to start Starbucks and Michael Dell to start Dell.

Enter our friend Saras D. Sarasvathy, professor at the University of Virginia's Darden School of Business. (We are huge fans of Sarasvathy's work. To connect with what she has written, see the Further Reading section at the end of the book.) Early in her work, she made a fascinating discovery, one that ran counter to the conventional wisdom. Sarasvathy studied serial entrepreneurs, people who have started two or more companies successfully.

But instead of looking at the behavior of entrepreneurs—which is indeed unique—Sarasvathy focused on how they think. There she found amazing similarities in how they reasoned, approached obstacles, and took advantage of opportunities. Yes, of course, there were variations. But the basic approach, as she understood it, was always the same.

In the face of an unknown future, entrepreneurs act. More specifically, they:

1.  Take a small, smart step (see "What's a Smart Step?") forward;

2.  Pause to see what they learned by doing so; and

3.  Build that learning into what they do next.

This process of act, learn, build, as we came to think about it, repeats until entrepreneurs are happy with the result, or they decide that they don't want to (or can't afford to) continue. At about this same time Sarasvathy was pursuing her research, the faculty at Babson started going down the same path and came to many of the same conclusions.

Inspired by all the research, we began to extend it in a variety of ways. We tested our ideas with colleagues and held more than two dozen seminars at which we invited smart, skeptical people to

## What's a Smart Step?

In our description of how Creaction works, we said that you take "smart steps" toward what you want, toward what you desire. So, what's a smart step?

It is the action you take based on the resources you have at hand and never involves more than you can afford to lose, that is, your acceptable loss. It can involve bringing other people along, although initially it does not have to.

Having taken the step, you pause to reflect on what you have learned. From there, you take another smart step or quit if your desire has waned (or you have discovered something else that you want more) or if you have exceeded your acceptable loss.

You repeat this process until:

1. You succeed. Or

2. You no longer want to continue. (You changed your mind; something else is more appealing.) Or

3. You exceed your acceptable loss. Or

4. You prove to yourself it can't be done.

challenge our framework's conclusions. They helped us refine and clarify our thinking, but our central findings only grew stronger as they told us about their experiences, which reinforced what we had learned.

So, we began to wonder if the way entrepreneurs think would work for the rest of us. Before moving on, we want to note a couple of things about that statement.

First, while we will use many business examples throughout the book, we will also be providing some that come from everyday life. This is not a business book in the traditional sense. (See "What You Won't See in This Book.")

## What You Won't See in This Book

1. **Only business examples.** Of course, there will be some business examples. We are business executives who have run and consulted with companies and taught this stuff as well. But you are also going to find examples from everyday life, since what we are advocating will work everywhere, not just in the office.

2. **An all-out attack on the way you were taught to think.** Invariably, when presenting a new approach to solving problems, authors go to great lengths to show why everything written before their work has been a waste of time. That's just silly. We are *not* going to say that the way you were taught to think was wrong. But we *are* going to say that there is another (and better) approach to use when confronting an unknown future.

   However, that does not mean you should use this new approach, which we have dubbed Creaction, exclusively. We will show how Creaction can work extremely well in conjunction with the way you already approach solving problems.

3. **Randomness.** When asked to summarize the central message of the book, we respond, "Action trumps everything." Some people hear that and think we are advocating "ready, fire, aim" or "leap before you look." We're not. In fact, we have applied, if you will, the business version of the scientific method, the process by which scientists, collectively and over time, try to create an accurate picture of the world. The steps they use are similar to those we are advocating: they ask a question or encounter a surprise ("I wonder . . . ?" "How come . . . ?"); do some research (we advocate doing just enough, but we do argue for doing it); construct a hypothesis; test the hypothesis (which in our case occurs by acting); and draw a conclusion based on what happens.

   In business today, you are often told to "experiment" in order to help shape an uncertain future. Creaction gives you the formula to do just that, a formula grounded in one of the best ways of conducting those experiments: the scientific method.

4. **Footnotes and other bits of professor-itis.** Although our approach is steeped in the scientific method, this is not going to be a textbook. We have great respect for academics. One of us is a university president who taught for more than two decades at the Harvard Business School. And as you will see (in "Further Reading"), our arguments are deeply grounded in academic research by dozens of people, including a Nobel Prize winner. But footnotes are distracting at best. We believe what we have to say is important and can literally change your life, and we know it can be said simply and directly.

Second, when we set out to see if the way serial entrepreneurs think would work for everyone, we weren't looking to replace Prediction. There were two reasons we weren't.

- As we have seen, Prediction works really well when the future can realistically be expected to be similar to the past, and since we are advocating smart steps (see sidebar), it certainly isn't smart to discard something that works well in a specific situation.

- Sarasvathy's research—which we will refer to throughout— shows that entrepreneurs continue to use Prediction effectively in the situations where it works well, that is, in the places where it is logical to assume that the future will be a lot like what has come before.

So, we were *not* looking to replace Prediction. Rather, we wanted to know whether the logic entrepreneurs employ when they face the unknown—we came to think of it as Creaction—would work for everyone else when the future is essentially unknowable. In other words, we wanted to know if Creaction could be used to complement Prediction in everyday situations that we frequently find ourselves in ("Can I convince the town to add a bicycle lane downtown?" "Will anyone buy what I have to sell, if I start a company?" "Would I be happy chucking it all to join the Peace Corps?")

We found that the entrepreneurial logic works in business and potentially elsewhere. You can use this way of thinking to complement the kind of reasoning you have already been taught—an additional way of thinking that can help you deal with high levels of uncertainty no matter what kind of situation you face.

## What are we are talking about?

What exactly is Creaction? Well, to start, it is based on *acting* and *creating* evidence, as contrasted with *thinking* and *analysis*.

Here's one way to think about that pivotal difference. A dancer dances. Substituting thinking for dancing doesn't work. If all you do is think, you end up just thinking about dancing. There is nothing to show for that thought.

Thinking is often a part of creating, but without action, nothing is created. This is true for even very intellectual, cerebral fields. For a task to be considered creating, you must publish, teach, or whatever. Daydreaming by itself is not creating.

How does Creaction play out in practice? How does it help us deal with uncertainty? The process has three parts, which repeat until you have reached your goal or decide you no longer want to. (See figure 1-1.)

1. **Desire.** Find or think of something you want. As we will discuss in chapter 2, you don't need a lot of passion; you only need sufficient desire to get started. ("I really want to start a restaurant, but I haven't a clue if I will ever be able to open one.")

FIGURE 1-1

**Creaction: How to act in uncertainty**

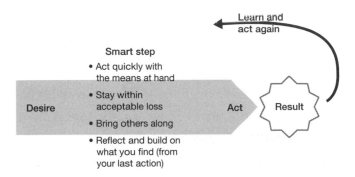

2.  **Take a smart step as quickly as you can.** As you will see, a smart step has its own three-part logic as well.

    - **Act quickly with the means at hand**—i.e. what you know, who you know, and anything else that's available. ("I know a great chef, and if I beg all my family and friends to back me, I might have enough money to open a place.")

    - **Stay within your acceptable loss.** Make sure the cost of that smart step (in terms of time, money, reputation, and so on) is never more than you are willing to lose should things not work out.

    - **Bring others along** to acquire more resources; spread the risk, and confirm the quality of your idea.

3.  **Build** on what you have learned from taking that step. Every time you act, reality changes. If you pay attention, you learn something from taking a smart step. More often than not, it gets you close to what you want. ("I should

be able to afford something just outside of downtown.") Sometimes what you want changes. ("It looks like there are an awful lot of Italian restaurants nearby. We are going to have to rethink our menu.") After you act, ask did those actions get me closer to my goal? ("Yes. It looks like I will be able to open a restaurant.") Do you need additional resources to draw even closer? ("Yes. I'll need to find another chef. The one I know can only do Italian.") Do you still want to obtain your objective? ("Yes.") Then act again and again until, building on what you learned, you have what you want (or you have decided you don't want it or you want something else instead).

---

Researchers found that successful entrepreneurs used a common logic that allows them to deal with situations in which the future is unpredictable. What works for them will work for you.

---

In other words, when facing the unknown, act your way into the future that you desire; don't think your way into it. Thinking does not change reality, nor does it necessarily lead to any learning. You can think all day about starting that restaurant, but thinking alone is not going to get you any closer to having one.

## Déjà vu all over again?

Sometimes, when we explain the concept of Creaction, people say it sounds familiar. It should; it was the way we all learned—at first.

## Thirteen Reasons Why Action Trumps Everything When the Future Is Unpredictable

Action, the cornerstone of Creaction, does indeed trump everything *when the future can't be known with much certainty*. That simple statement makes sense, of course. If you are heading into an unknown frontier—and starting a new journey of any sort usually qualifies—the only way to really discover what is out there is to go and find out. "Are there potential customers?" "Is  the market big enough?" "Will the community like the civic venture I helped create?" Take a small, smart step and find out. Thinking and creating endless "what if" scenarios doesn't help you. You can "what if" yourself to death. The only way to know for sure is to act, reflect on what you have learned, and act some more to gain more learning.

But before you do, double-check to see that the future is as uncertain as you think; that there is, indeed, no way to predict what will happen. If there is a more than reasonable chance that the future *is* knowable, you are often better off letting Prediction dominate, and that is a good thing.

Remember what we said at the beginning. Prediction and Creaction frequently work in tandem and each works better in certain situations. You could take an egg out of the refrigerator, hold it out at arm's length, and, to find out what will happen if you drop it, take action by letting go. But there is little reason for doing so (other than to entertain a three-year-old). The laws of gravity are well known. You can predict the fact that the egg will break with near certainty.

Similarly, you could go out and start a transportation company tomorrow and learn as you go how many cars, trucks, motorcycles, and bicycles you can sell in a given year, then sort those numbers by categories—coupes, convertibles, SUVs, and so on—and chart sales during good economic times and bad. But there is no reason to go through all that effort and risk. Those numbers are readily available, and you can estimate future transportation sales with reasonable confidence.

Our point is simple: when the results of thinking would lead to actions that are predictable ("I wonder how many high-end sports cars I could sell in a year during an economic slump"), let predictive thinking dominate, supplementing it with Creaction as necessary. You can expect Prediction to give you a solid result, that is, you know the uncooked egg will crack when it hits the floor, and you can come up with numbers that will project fairly accurately how many specific types of cars you are likely to sell in a given period.

But in the face of unknowability—what is the market for motorized skateboards with training wheels or for a four-wheel Segway, things that don't yet exist—you can't do a lot of learning in advance. In this case, the fastest, easiest, most effective (and often only) way to get that learning is by acting.

Here are thirteen reasons why:

1. **If you act, you will find out what works . . .**

2. **. . . and what doesn't.**

3. **If you never act, you will never know what is possible and what is not.** You may *think* you know, but you won't be able to point to anything concrete to prove you are right. The problem with that, as Mark Twain famously pointed out, is clear: "It ain't so much the things we don't know that get us into trouble. It's the things we know that just ain't so."

4. **If you act, you will find out if you like it** . . . with "it" being whatever the new action is . . .

5. **. . . or you don't.**

6. **Acting leads to a market reaction, which could point you in another direction.** You thought you were going to open the world's best Italian restaurant. Taking a small step toward that goal, you began hosting large dinner parties and cooking for the monthly meeting of the Elks club to try out your recipes and discover firsthand what the food service business is like. People raved about your food, but were surprised when you

didn't want to talk to them. You, in turn, were left cold by the experience. You hated interacting with people; the idea of doing all the logistics necessary (finding a place, dealing with the constant turnover of waitstaff, etc.) made you break out in a cold sweat, and you really didn't want to prepare more than three kinds of entrées at a time. It turns out you learned that you liked the cooking part of running a restaurant but weren't crazy about all the rest. Your action, the decision to take steps toward starting a restaurant caused a market reaction. People loved the food but found you to be a cold fish; you loved the cooking but could do without everything else. Your action has convinced you to go into high-end catering and hire someone to deal with the clients.

7. **As you act, you can find people to come along with you.** For example, in talking to your suppliers, you ended up meeting the world's most organized person. She now runs the day-to-day operations of your catering business and is a 10 percent owner.

8. **As you act, you can find ways to do things faster, cheaper, better.** You discover, after making your world-famous chicken parmesan fifty times, that you can prepare the dish in eight steps instead of eleven.

9. **If you act, you won't spend the rest of your life going, "I wonder what would have happened if . . ."**

10. **If all you do is think, you may end up being less interesting as a person.** Who would you rather sit next to on a plane, someone who started a successful rock-climbing store (or even an unsuccessful one), or someone who only thought about it?

11. **If all you ever do is think about stuff,** you can gain tons of theoretical knowledge, but none from the real world. You become like that woman in the fable who knows the price of

everything but the value of nothing. In other words, if all you ever do is think . . . all you do is think.

12. **Action always leads to evidence.** You act, therefore something changes, and in observing that reaction, you gain knowledge. ("Hmm, if I drop an egg from shoulder height, it shatters.") Thinking doesn't lead to proof—or messy floors. As Scott Cook, the founder of Intuit, said when interviewed for a *Harvard Business Review* article: "Evidence is better than anyone's intuition."

13. **If you act, you know what is real.** You always want to know what's real.

For all these reasons and dozens more that you can come up with on your own, action trumps everything when the future is highly uncertain.

When you were a child, everything was unknown or uncertain, so you started learning through action. You'd make a sound and something happened; your mother responded. You pulled the cat's tail and got scratched. So, what we advocate amounts to the recovery of a skill we all had a long time ago: *the ability to act your way into better thinking.*

Remember, Creaction complements Prediction. When Prediction makes sense, predict. When it doesn't, think about using Creaction.

As you deal with a new situation, you will invariably bounce back and forth between the two. That is exactly what you should do. In fact, we have a term for the process of using both forms of reasoning: Entrepreneurial Thought and Action. That's our phrase for using *both* Prediction and Creaction together to solve a problem or create something new.

## Creaction: One Person's Story

No one's journey is typical. But how Jodi Rosenbaum brought More Than Words (MTW) into being represents how Creaction works.

MTW, as its Web site explains, "is a nonprofit social enterprise that empowers youth who are in the foster care system, court involved, homeless, or out of school to take charge of their lives by taking charge of a business. By working as a team to manage their own retail and online book business, café and community space, they develop the employment skills, leadership, and self-confidence they need to successfully transition to adulthood."

The MTW approach is clearly working: some 35 percent of the youth have some sort of court involvement—an open charge or restrictions put on them by the Massachusetts Division of Youth and Family Services—when they start work at MTW. That number drops to 9 percent when they stop working there and is at 4 percent after twenty-four months. Some 85 percent go on to earn their GED or high school diploma.

Let's look at how the four parts of Creaction played out, in Rosenbaum's words:

**Desire.** "My background is in child welfare and the juvenile justice system as a child advocate. I have over 15 years of experience with how young people often don't have the opportunities, accountability and support to really move their lives forward and fulfill their potential.

"Seven years ago I was working with youth development programs through Harvard [where she earned her master's] and I wanted to get back involved with the foster care system and I was also interested in business and the concept of social enterprise using business to help deliver on a mission. But I didn't quite know how it all meshed together."

**Starting with the means at hand.** "There was no grand vision. One day my best friend found a pile of books set out for garbage.

She brought them home and looked them up online and saw they were actually worth some money. We looked at each other and said wow this could work!" Specifically, Rosenbaum thought she could have young, at-risk people figure out how to price the books and sell and deliver them. "We could use the revenue that comes in to help pay for this hands-on, real-world learning and training experience. This would be a really good vehicle for teens. It would help them gain skills and be empowered, productive and engaged in a job and their lives."

**Taking a smart step within the bounds of your acceptable loss.** Rosenbaum kept her day job while researching the online used-book market, and eventually opened MTW in a 150-square-foot space with an inventory of donated books.

**Reflecting and building on what she found (part I).** There was a market and the young people who worked at MTW realized that the more effort they put in, the more they got out of the experience in terms of business knowledge, technology and financial skills, and, as Rosenbaum points out, "they learned the critical life skills of showing up on time and of working as a team, and communicating, and making eye contact."

**Reflecting and building on what she found (part II).** "I did a lot of cold calling to get additional financial support for some of the operating expenses because the revenue from the books didn't cover the entire budget. Our first corporate supporter was Boston Scientific. I got the right person at the right time on the phone and she 'got' what we were trying to do. She said they just weren't sure they could be the first on board but to keep them posted on how I was doing. Then we got a small grant from the Executive Office of Public Safety. Somebody there had read a concept paper I had written and liked it and reached out to us. We wound up getting funded for an intervention for reducing crime and supporting some of our most at-risk young people.

I took that back to Boston Scientific and they immediately pulled the trigger and wrote a check. Once I had them, I had leverage to go to others since I was able to say we have government sponsorship *and* we have a corporate source."

**Building (part III).** "The young people experienced success and it bred success. The more they sold a great book for $40, the more they wanted to find good books to sell to make money. Within a year's time we were signing the lease on a retail storefront, and we added a café."

## About the journey ahead

As you have already seen, we are big believers in practicing what we preach. We continued that approach in how we constructed this book. We will:

1. Help you take small, smart steps.

2. Pause to review what you've learned, and then

3. Move ahead, building on that knowledge.

You have just started part I, "What to Do When Facing the Unknown," which deals with the two foundations of Creaction: uncertainty, in chapter 1, and desire, in chapter 2.

In part II, we will cover the four individual elements that make up the logic of Creaction, and in part III, we will show in detail how to apply Creaction in certain situations (in large organizations or with family and friends). We will conclude by coming full circle and explain how entrepreneurs have proven this method works—not only for them, but for all of us. You will find that discussion in chapter 10 and the epilogue.

## That's all there is

There you have it. That's our book in a nutshell. We set out to answer one simple question: what do you do when the way you think doesn't allow you to thrive in today's brave new world? We think we have developed an answer that will allow you to succeed in the face of uncertainty.

---

### If you have insufficient data, make your own.

---

If you find the idea appealing, in the pages ahead, you will find a detailed description of how to use Creaction in all kinds of situations you may encounter at work and in your personal life.

If you don't, well, you found out how the approach works. You took a small step into the unknown (learning about Creaction) and decided it's not for you. That learning was worthwhile, too.

Incidentally, although there is tons of research that support the ideas and arguments we will present (see the Further Reading section at the end of the book), if you get some value out of this book, it will *not* be because we convinced you with these arguments. It will be because what we have to say resonates with what you already know. It will strike you as common sense. To find out if it does, turn the page. The journey is about to begin for real.

## Takeaways

1. **When the future is unknowable,** how we traditionally reason is extremely limited in predicting what will happen. You need to complement the way you were taught to reason with a new kind of thinking: Creaction.

2. **Creaction does *not* replace prediction reasoning;** it works with it. One is not necessarily better than the other (it depends on the circumstance), but using them together is a very effective prescription.

3. **If Creaction feels familiar,** and it should, that is because it is the way we reason naturally. All we are advocating is rediscovering a skill you already have.

# 2

# The Overwhelming
# Importance of Desire

Unless you truly want to make something happen, the odds
are nothing will. Without desire, nothing else matters ... or occurs. So, the starting point is: what do you want to create?

YOU HAVE SOME SORT OF IDEA of what you'd like to bring
into being. That concept could be as vague as "I want to do
something to make people healthier," or as specific as creating a new
initiative at work. Maybe it doesn't have anything to do with commerce. It could be for a nonprofit that can bridge racial differences or
an outreach program for kids.

Each and every one of those ideas could be great, but you need to
do something to make them a reality. As we said, thinking is terrific, but absolutely nothing happens unless you take smart steps to
translate your idea into action. You need to discover if you are right
about there being a potential audience or customer for your ideas
(and learn what you need to change if there is not).

So far, so good. But what causes people to act? We need to know
why some people feel compelled to move from thinking to doing, a
step that the rest of the world—those folks who *think* they have a

good idea for a book, nonprofit, Web site, retail concept, new initiative at work, or civic initiative—never make.

## Going right to the source

If you ask entrepreneurs of any stripe what made them get started, you will get widely diverse answers: "I always knew I wanted to do this," "I sort of stumbled into it," "I wanted to make a lot of money, and this idea was the way to do it," "I never really cared about making a lot of money. This was a way to help people."

But if you search for commonality, it is easy to find. They *wanted* to do it; often they say they had to do it; they felt compelled. To reduce it to a word, what caused them to act was *desire*. They had a desire—sometimes an overwhelming desire, but always, at the very least, a desire—to act, to create something. Now it could have been a desire to get away from something they didn't like—"I just can't stand working for anyone else"—but it is desire nonetheless. (We will talk about desires like this later.)

Desire is a word people rarely use in connection with commerce. When it surfaces, some people are quick to try to eliminate it because it sounds squishy, unbusinesslike, and, of course, hard to quantify and teach. But it is the right word to use here, defined as "a longing or craving, as for something that brings satisfaction or enjoyment." Its synonyms are even more accurately descriptive: aspiration, longing, passion, and yearning, language that—as the *Random House Dictionary of the English Language* correctly points out—"suggests feelings that impel one to the attainment or possession of something . . . that is (in reality or imagination) within reach." Desire is what compels people to create something new, something that they want to bring into being.

## Desire Inside Large Organizations

Desire is a motivating force for creation no matter where you look—even inside a *Fortune* 300 company. Meet Noah McIntyre.

I was hired at Whole Foods as a buyer and that sort of didn't work out. It wasn't what I grooved on. It was too much dealing with stuff and not enough dealing with people. My real passion is to interact with people at work and talk about health and nutrition. So I was able to figure out a new role for myself which was pretty much self-created.

I proposed this to my boss. I said let me do more marketing and more food demonstrations. She said sure. We have this huge stack of protein powders we need to sell. I said great; I can make smoothies out of that. And I'll add other higher-end vitamins so people can see how you can add all your vitamins to one drink and they will also buy the higher-margin vitamins.

Twice a week, the store manager sets up food demonstrations in every department, and Monday nights was like the budget night where we show the inexpensive products and Friday night is the night we show the more gourmet products, so I tied the smoothies into what was going on with the promotions. I did the store-brand protein on Mondays and the higher-end gourmet designer sports nutrition drinks on Friday nights.

I did this for about three months, and the store-brand protein powder became a huge best-seller. And now I have a standing gig of doing smoothie bars on Monday and Friday. It is so cool.

And it was because McIntyre had a desire to do something different and not do something that he didn't groove on.

In Creaction, two things are always present, uncertainty and desire. We have already talked at length about uncertainty. Now we'll look at desire in more detail, explaining not only what it is, but also how and why it governs Creaction.

## Passionate about why passion isn't necessarily necessary

Let's begin by dealing with a misconception. When people think about desire, they almost automatically equate it with passion, as in the passion entrepreneurs have in starting their business. And they conclude that this passion is an absolute requirement before getting underway. Indeed, how many times have you heard this advice given to people thinking of starting a company: "You've got to be passionate about it. You gotta love what you do."

We are here to tell you it ain't necessarily so. If what you mean by passion is a deep, personal commitment, then yes, having passion is a good thing. Having strong positive emotions about your venture is an asset for obvious reasons: You are more likely to get started. You are more likely to persist. You are more likely to be creative in solving the problems you encounter.

But if by passion, you mean blinding, manic focus, ignoring everything and anything that gets in your way, that's not such a good idea. It's actually a destructive force. People destroy and kill out of passion. Moreover, it leads to misperceptions of reality. The best thing we can say about products such as Smith and Wesson Mountain Bikes, Colgate Kitchen Entrees, and Thirsty Dog and Thirsty Cat (designer water for pets) is that the people who brought them to market must have been blinded by their passion for the idea.

So from now on, let's use the term passion in a positive sense: emotionally stirring, like love or yearning. Even then, passion is not a requirement.

"But," you might say, "all the interviews with people who have had huge market successes always talk about the passion they have about these ventures."

Yes, but they probably didn't have it at the beginning. Honest. Listen to what David Friedman of Boston Logic Technology Partners told us:

> My cofounder Matt Weiss and I were housemates in college and we said to each other, "Someday we are going to start a company together." When we first launched Boston Logic, we actually started an entirely different company, a technology one, wrote a business plan, and sought venture capital, just like everyone said we should. It went nowhere.
>
> So there we were. Two friends sitting in a leased office going nowhere. So, we took on some consulting work in the real estate brokerage world, and we started to see all sorts of opportunities to provide online marketing and Web design services to our clients to help them find and service home buyers, renters, and sellers. After a couple of years, we converted our consulting solutions into software products and discovered how much more profitable and scalable they were than billable-day work.
>
> We've continued a version of that formula to this day. Every quarter, we compare what our clients have asked for, what they are using, and what we want to do. Based on these factors, and the effort required to build each feature, we select which upgrades we want to offer to our users and which new features or new products we want to try selling.
>
> We're constantly saying, "Here are all the opportunities. Here's what we know to be true and what we know how to do. Based on that understanding and our resources, here's what we chose to do." Sometimes, we develop features that almost no one ends up using. But you're making decisions and your attitude is, I want to decide something relatively quickly that

doesn't cost too much and get started. We're deciding and acting quickly. A one-hour meeting decides ninety days of development priorities. We know some of them aren't going to work, but we'll get further ahead by deciding small things and moving and correcting our mistakes than if we sit and think about things too much.

Friedman, who now serves as the president and CEO, tells us, "Matt and I were gung-ho about building a successful company with customers who love our products. We started out towards one goal, and then made a left turn. And ended up completely in love with what we're doing now."

We heard that sort of story time after time. Are people who are running successful companies passionate about them now? Yes. Were they that way at the beginning? Often, as Friedman did, they just stumbled into them. So thinking you have to be passionate can take you down a wrong road.

While passion at inception isn't necessary, desire is. It's all-important to any innovative endeavor. Creators and entrepreneurs are always doing what they want or something that will get them to what they want. But that's more or less true for all of us. It's no secret that people are motivated and driven by desire and Friedman and Weiss certainly had a desire to create something and be in business together.

Desire in any creative endeavor is like falling in love. Some of us, maybe you, were smitten at first sight, falling instantly and passionately in love on that enchanted evening as you gazed across a crowded room. That happens to *some* entrepreneurs, too. They fall hopelessly in love the second they think of the concept. But we will bet that happens as rarely as finding in high school the person you are going to spend the rest of your life with. For most of us, falling in love occurs over time. You date, go steady, get married, and grow more deeply in love as life goes on. Desire is like that. More often than not, it builds over time. Of course, this is as true for anyone else as it is for entrepreneurs who are pursuing something that matters to them.

So it's not that the entrepreneurs, or the other people who are successful, are lying when they talk about their passion in the magazine articles or books you read about them. At the time those things were written, they *were* passionate. *But that passion was not necessarily present at inception.* In fact, in one study of fifty entrepreneur partnerships, forty-two found partners before they had the idea, just as in Friedman and Weiss's case.

---

### If you believe that passion and desire must be in place before you act, you may never start.

---

Even if passion is required, it is of no practical use to know that. You cannot synthesize or fake desire. When was the last time you tried to want something you didn't want, or love someone you didn't love? You can't manipulate yourself into caring. While in the rare case we can be instantaneously smitten (the birth of a child), more often we come to care about things or people over time (our best friends). In either case, desire is not something that we self-consciously create; it is something that we are gifted with. Telling someone that he has to be passionate about something is worthless advice because he can't do anything about it.

If you are smitten by an idea, follow your bliss! But don't fall prey to the impression that you'd better not start that new venture unless you are passionate about it. It's far better to get started with whatever desire you have.

# Types of desire

Let's deconstruct desire a bit to better understand it. The real drivers of our behavior are *emotional* desires, things we pursue because of the *feeling*, often of pleasure or wholeness that is anticipated if we can fulfill them. We generally don't know where our emotional desires come from or why. They mostly seem to overtake us, often for no reason whatsoever. We want "it" deeply because we *want* it. Desires seem and can often be irrational, and mostly, we don't get to choose them.

Intellectual desires, by contrast, are constructed by our rational mind. They are reasoned and make logical sense. You can explain them and they are immediately understandable to others.

Here's the big point, and you already know it. While in the short term, an intellectual desire can win battles with an emotional desire, in the long term, emotional desires carry the day. Michael Crichton was trained as physician, but he "had" to become a writer. Countless creators of popular music had other careers at first. Cole Porter, Arthur Schwartz, and Hogey Carmichael were originally lawyers, for example. We get the most creative when pursuing things we care about, and as we will discuss next, persistence is natural.

## A deeper dive

When a desire's primary function is to help fulfill another desire, we can term it "instrumental." Instrumental desires generally lead to desires of increasing importance. The desire for success on a particular project leads to success in your job. Success at your job leads to career advancement. Career advancement leads to security.

In contrast, "terminal" desires, such as security, are ends unto themselves (you don't want it because you expect it to lead to something else), and most terminal desires are pretty emotional.

Since desire is the fuel for Creaction, whatever instrumental desire is in front of you right now, you want to be able to connect it to a terminal desire if you can because, as we said, terminal desires can be particularly powerful.

In fact, some terminal desires are so powerful that we need another term for them altogether. And it's a word even more unfamiliar in business than desire. That word is *love*.

## Love

Love, as we define it, is the yearning for the realization of what you seek to create *on its own terms*. Love is caring enough about the creation that you will do what it takes for it to become real. To be sure, success will lead to your own happiness but is often wanted for the sake of the thing itself.

Love is the relationship that many artists have with their specific works. Over time, the central question becomes, "What does this work need?" in contrast with, "What do I want to do next?" The love of the creation drives the choices that are made, and what is required is much clearer and undistorted. (It's no longer about you, it's about *it*.)

Some entrepreneurs achieve this relationship with their ventures. Like their children, they give birth and rear them, and like their children, their ventures have lives of their own. As the poet Khalil Gibran wrote:

> *They come through you but not from you,*
> *And though they are with you yet they belong not to you.*
> *You may give them your love but not your thoughts,*
> *For they have their own thoughts.*

## Persistence and commitment

An essential characteristic of entrepreneurs is perseverance: the ability to picture and maintain focus on what they are trying to create, dropping anything that distracts from or interferes with that focus. Holding something in your imagination is extremely challenging when you're relying upon your intellect, telling yourself it is a good idea or that you should keep at it. But it is unavoidable if it's something that you actually love.

Think about the last time you were in love. It was impossible not to think about the loved one. Think about your children. How many times a day do you think about their well-being?

Love of the venture has the same power. Focusing attention on what you want to create and dropping anything that distracts you are the most natural things in the world when you are emotionally stirred by love, or passion, or whatever term you might prefer.

When you have the desire to do something, you become committed. Behaviorally, commitment is simply cropping out the thought that distracts you from what you have promised yourself you will do. You say you are committed to X, and then Y comes along. You pay it no heed and return your attention to X. Y announces itself again. And again you ignore it. The process happens over and over again until Y (and Z and A and B . . .) gives up, leaving you to concentrate on what you want to create.

## What makes people pull the trigger?

So we now have a handle on desire, but desire in and of itself doesn't seem to be enough to get people moving. All those people who have an idea for a book, new invention, or retail concept that they are willing to talk to you about at a party presumably really do want to pursue that idea. And all those people who *know* they have an idea for an actual better mousetrap say they want to make it a reality. So, why don't they? When does the desire become so strong that you have to act on it?

The answer boils down to this: when you want something, have the means at hand to get it, and the next step is within your acceptable loss, the most natural thing in the world is to act. In fact, it's almost unnatural not to.

Of course, you can also be motivated to move away from something, which is the negative side of the coin. There the motivation goes: no matter how scary or unsettling starting a new venture may be, the alternative of doing nothing is worse. Your current situation makes it imperative for you to do something else, but while it may be sufficient to get you started, as we will see, this will probably not work as a motivating force in the long term. (More on this in a moment.)

---

Desire is the most critical resource you have in starting a new venture. Why? Because it:
- Motivates you to act.
- Enables you to persist.
- Makes you more creative (especially in the face of obstacles).

---

With the framework established, let's look at desire in more detail, because as we said, if the desire isn't there, odds are nothing new is going to be created.

Let's start with the positive desires.

## "What if . . .?"

When inspiration strikes, it is always unique, but the spark that gets people to act is always familiar. They say to themselves: "I wonder what would happen if . . . ?" or "It might be fun to . . ." or "I bet if I did . . . , it would bring me . . . " or "This idea has me by the throat and I need to do something with it to see how it plays out."

Whether the idea is all-encompassing ("It has me by the throat") or appears as an entertaining notion ("Wouldn't it be fun if . . . ?"), the person is intrigued enough or compelled to take action. We aren't talking about people selling everything they own and going into the new venture whole hog. They have no intention of quitting their day jobs and spending every waking moment on making this new thing a reality. (See our discussion of entrepreneurial myths in chapter 3.) Rather, they are thinking, "Let me take a first step and see what happens. And if I like the results, I'll keep going."

Put differently, they don't see a lot of downside in getting underway. Think about all the people who created dot-coms during the late 1990s and into the early 2000s. Invariably, when asked whether they found the idea of starting their own company risky, they said something like, "If it doesn't work out, I can always go back to what I was doing." The cynics will point out that a lot of those people did end up going back to their former sources of employment once the tech bubble burst. To which we say, true, but an awful lot of companies that got started then are still up and running. As the Kauffman Foundation, which is devoted to promoting entrepreneurship and innovation, points out, between 1980 and 2005, virtually all new jobs in the United States—about 40 million in total—were created by firms that were five years old or less. Netting out layoffs, retirements, and the number of people who moved from one big company to another, established firms did not create a single job. It was all those new companies that survived that did.

## "Get me out of here"

On the other hand, the negative desires are easy to understand as well. People sometimes start a business because their current situation feels or truly is awful, and they can't stand the status quo. They are working at a job they despise; they desperately need more money; they simply hate the answer they give when someone asks, "What do you do to make a living?" You get the idea. Anything, even plunging into the unknown, is better than what they are doing now.

Getting rid of something you don't want can be a great spur to action. It can get you going in another direction. But the problem is that it is not great enough to sustain you over time. It's like lighting a fire under yourself (or having one lit). Once you get far enough away, then the heat is off and the impetus wanes. You've got to relight the fire or find someone or something else to prod you into action. This is a lot of work and more than a bit self-abusive.

It is always more desirable to move toward something you truly want than to move away from something you hate, or to move toward something that strikes you as a good idea but you don't really care about it. This is because when you're doing something that you want, the quality of energy you bring to the activity is entirely different than when you are doing something you feel obligated to do, or something that is simply a (slightly) better alternative than the awful status quo you face.

While desperation can get you started, at some point, if fleeing a negative situation is why you have chosen to create something new, the switch will have to flip. You will have to truly want to continue working on the idea, otherwise you probably will lose the motivation to see it through, and ironically you could end up in exactly the same place you started, hating how you are spending your days. There are exceptions. There are people who succeed in order "to show everyone who said I couldn't that they were wrong." However, those people tend to be (a) rare and (b) not always very happy, despite their success.

## Why desire is so important

There are four questions you might ask before starting any new venture:

1. Is it feasible, that is, is it within the realm of reality?

2. Can I do it, that is, is it feasible for me?

3. Is it worth doing? Will there be a market for what I want to sell? Is there potential to turn a profit? Will people appreciate what I am trying to do? In other words, does it make sense to put in all this effort?

(Notice these first three questions are matters of predicting, which underscores the fact that Creaction and Prediction can and do work together.)

4. Do I want to do it?

This last question is the one that really matters: do you want to create the new venture?

Why is that pivotal? Either the venture is something that you want, or it's something that leads to something you want. If it is neither of these, there's no reason to act or to answer the other three questions. Creaction, by definition, applies when you personally care about what you are trying to create, and not necessarily anywhere else.

Now, if you *want* to create it, then in the known (Prediction-based) world, it can make sense to spend time and effort on questions one, two, and three. But in the unknowable world, where you can't predict the future, the answers to the first three questions are all the same: "There is no way of telling." You won't know until you actually try. You can do all the market research you want, ask everyone what they think about your idea, or speculate endlessly. But the only way to truly discover if there is gold at the end of the rainbow is to take an action and see what happens. Until you act, you won't know.

However, none of that matters until—and unless—you answer the fourth question: do I want to do it? There is simply no way you are going to give the venture your full effort if your heart isn't in it at least to some degree.

## The role of desire in assessing risk

Once you want to do something, everything gets reframed. The negative emotional response to all the unknowns is reduced. The reality hasn't changed. You still don't know what is out there, but you'll find a way around the problem, because you care about what you are trying to do.

Let's say you work for a farm machinery manufacturer, and your boss gives you the assignment of figuring out how to sell the company's products in Eastovia. Here's how our four questions play out:

**Is it feasible?** You haven't a clue how to set up a distribution and service network in an underdeveloped country or whether your equipment is suitable to its hilly terrain.

**Can you do it?** Maybe. Maybe not. You've never done anything like this before.

**Is it worth doing?** Who knows the size of the market and whether it will be profitable?

**Do you want to do it?** Well, no. It's the boss's idea.

Situation number two is exactly the same, but *you* are the one who wants to sell farm equipment in Eastovia. You think there is a huge opportunity and you have a compelling desire to give it a try, in no small part because your wife's family lives there.

What's the likely result in both cases? It isn't a hard question.

In the first situation, where desire is *not* part of the equation, you aren't in any hurry to do anything because the situation is so uncertain and unknown. You will keep thinking about what you are up against and search for more data. After all, it's better to study carefully and make sure all the bases are covered than to launch, have it not work out, and then have everyone say, "You didn't think it through." At best, you will take a lot of time, and at worst, you will put it at the very bottom of your to-do pile, never taking any real action and hoping your boss never follows up, even though the opportunity might have been real.

But the presence of desire alters all of that. Because you want to do it, you are much more likely to take a first, small, smart step toward dealing with the challenge. For example, the next time you and your wife are visiting her family, you stop in and see some local distributors and set up an exploratory meeting with the minister of agriculture's staff. And as we see in chapter 6, your passion for creating something new will make it far easier to get others to come along with you as either investors or employees. Nobody will be committed to what you're doing if they don't see your desire, your belief in your idea, and your willingness to try to accomplish it.

## When to stop and what happens if your desire wanes?

We've made the case that desire is critical. And odds are you will be filled with desire as you get underway in whatever new venture you start. But:

- You're working hard on something that you desire and hit a tough patch. How do you deal with the frustration?

- How do you stay in touch with the desire, while accepting that it will wax and wane?

- How do you know when it's just over?

These are related but quite different questions. Let's take them in order, starting with what you do when times are really tough.

Of course, anyone who has ever done something difficult has had moments of frustration, anger, disappointment, and even despair. But as Jimmy Dugan (the Tom Hanks character) in *A League of Their Own* says about playing women's professional baseball: "It's supposed to be hard. If it wasn't hard, everyone would do it. The hard . . . is what makes it great."

When you hit a bump or a slump, there are two things to remember. First is that whether your feelings have an impact on your ability to create what you want is entirely your option. It is true that repeated frustration and disappointment *can* erode desire, but they don't have to. Your ability to create what you want is not inherently affected by how you might feel. Remember all the great artists who had long bouts of misery on the way to creating their masterpieces.

It is the most natural thing for people to experience negative emotions when their desires are blocked. Ask any baby for confirmation. In these moments, or even long spells, we have this choice: we can reignite our creative power by reaffirming our desire for our vision or we can decide that our comfort and emotional state are more important than our vision. The easy and quick way to alleviate our negative emotions is to pretend that we don't want what we want or give up. We might think we feel better, but we won't get what we want that way. Still, the pain, frustration, or anger will go away. We say this with no prejudice; it is your choice whether to proceed or not.

Whether you choose comfort over desire or desire over comfort is totally your call.

As for the second question, how do you stay in touch with the desire, while accepting that it will wax and wane? Well, it would be nice to think that you will be ever more enthusiastic about your new venture as time goes on. But what happens if you are not? Is that a bad thing? Not necessarily. It's pretty normal.

The day-to-day reality of building a business or creating anything new can be wearing, so swings of enthusiasm are natural. This is one of the reasons why becoming fluent with the feeling of desire is so useful. At a particular moment in time, you may not be passionate. But do you still want it? If the answer is yes, then you should probably keep going, even if you decide to step away from the project for a few days, or even a few months. Taking a break is healthy, and it might help you gain perspective. When you resume, act, even if only for a few minutes each day. Acting in favor of your desires will build momentum, if it is to be built at all.

Which brings us to the question of how do you know when it's just over and the thing you thought you desired has been explored and found to be unachievable?

The same questions that got you started can give you insight into whether to stop. Assume you still have desire. Have you proved to yourself that it is impossible? Or that you simply can't do it; it's not in your makeup? Or that your idea, while possible, is simply not something that anyone else values? Or that to proceed requires you to spend or risk more time, money, or reputation than you want? (We'll have more to say on this subject in chapter 4.) If the answer to *any* of these questions is a truthful yes, it's an indicator that you should probably stop, maybe permanently or maybe only so long as that answer stays yes. After all, over time, technology, what you can do, and what others want can change. Just remember that the answers to these questions are all predictions and that in the face of the truly unknown, prediction is not reliable.

So the simple answer is that as long as you still have desire, persist, although you may want to rebalance your focus more on other desires that show more immediate promise, pushing this one toward the bottom of the list.

However, if the loss of desire seems permanent, it is time to do something else. Again, this is common, too. For example, we see it all the time with entrepreneurs who are full of desire when they are in the process of getting their companies up and running and then lose zeal when the firm is fully underway. When that happens, it is time for them to leave—either sell or turn the running of the company over to a professional manager—and do something else.

## One last situation

Maybe you say you don't have a clue what your desires are anymore, after sublimating them for so long. What can you do to get in touch with them again? The short answer is, once more, act.

Here's the longer answer, and it underscores why it is so important to become fluent with desire. Imagine that for the first twenty years of your life, things were mostly about you and getting what you want. Then you got married and had children. For the next thirty years of your life, it was no longer primarily about you getting what you wanted. You were now second and your life was about your family and getting what *they* wanted. Consider that thirty years of conditioning.

Now, you're an empty nester. For most of us, the transition back to the primacy of our own desires doesn't happen overnight. It requires time and practice. Get used to wanting things. What does it feel like? The feeling is different with things you *think* you want. Act in favor of the ones that feel like genuine desires. The more you practice, the faster it will magically sort itself out, and pretty quickly, too. You'll find that you haven't lost the capacity for desire. It's just been asleep.

## How desire flows through all of the other elements of Creaction

A bit of foreshadowing. The next four chapters will deal with the four logical elements that make up Creaction. Desire is central to all four. If we touch on those four cornerstones here, you can see why that is the case (and we won't have to risk boring you with a short sidebar in each of the next four chapters pointing out how desire is a vital part of what we are talking about).

**Act quickly with the means at hand.** Absent desire, in the face of uncertainty, it simply makes more sense to think, study, and predict. Why go into the unknown unless you want to? Desire is the force that gets you to take action.

**Assess your acceptable loss.** What you can spend may be fixed, but what you are *willing* to spend will change, based on desire. And if your limit is, indeed, actually fixed, desire makes it more likely you will be creative in finding new sources of assets.

**Build on what you find.** Desire keeps you moving. Otherwise, in the face of obstacles, it is easy to stop. Not only does desire give you the impetus to keep going, it will drive you to find ways around the problems. This is no guarantee of success, but it's the best you can do.

**Bring other people along.** No one will enroll unless you are committed, and obviously it is your desire that gets you to commit.

## Just Start:
## An Exercise for Finding Your Desire

Because desire is an intrinsic motivating force, sometimes you are not exactly clear about its specifics. (For example, yes, you know you want to help people, but which people and how?)

To help clarify your desire(s), write down a half-dozen things you want. Not ideals, obligations, or intellectually the right things to do, but things you desire.

Find a friend or two to engage in conversation about:

1.  A few of those things you each have on your list.

2.  Ask one another how each of you knows which one thing or things you desire most and how that desire makes you feel.

You will probably end up with a clearer picture of what you desire.

## Takeaways

1.  **Nothing happens until you take that first smart step.**  All the ideas in the world don't mean a thing unless you do something with them. If you don't act, all you have is a bunch of ideas.

2.  **But before you act . . . you need to know what _you_ want.**  If you don't eventually develop a strong desire, odds are you will never see your idea through.

3.  **You don't need to be obsessed or even in love with the idea,** but there must be some reason pushing you forward. Otherwise, nothing will happen.

*Part Two*

# What to Do When You Take Action in the Face of Uncertainty

# 3

# Act Quickly with the Means at Hand

Entrepreneurs love reality. They always want to be standing on firm ground. So does anyone who wants to create something new or anyone setting out into the unknown for that matter. That just makes sense. You always want to know exactly where you are.

So the ability to take stock of current reality is incredibly important, as we will see in the next four chapters. That is especially true with this one. You want to know exactly what assets you have at your disposal—and what you don't. It is the first of the four fundamental building blocks of Creaction. And once you have taken stock of that inventory, you need to act.

ENTREPRENEURS create new businesses and new business models in much the same way as anyone else professionally engaged in the creation of new things. *Professional creator* is an equal if not better description for the entrepreneur than *businessperson*, since entrepreneurs bring new businesses into being in much the same manner as a composer who creates a new choral work. Or a software engineer who creates a new program or computer game. Or a writer who creates a book. Or a marketer who creates a new ad campaign. Where there was nothing before—a blank canvas—something is created, a choral work, software program, new computer game, novel, or ad.

You can use the creative process to bring into being almost anything you desire. And as we saw in the last chapter, the creative process begins with that desire. You want what you want, but you don't yet have it. So you go off to create it.

Thus, the two major elements to the creative process are the "want" (desire) and the "don't have" (current reality). The space between the two sets up a tension that drives action and invention as creators strive to close the gap between what they want and what they currently have.

Experienced creators understand that for the process to work well you need the creative tension. You must have a sufficiently clear vision of what you want and a very clear perception of current reality (in this case, what you don't have). Without both, you have no creative tension.

Experienced creators are fine with getting started with a less-than-complete vision of what they want because they know that they will clarify it as they move along. "I want to do something to help children" might turn into "starting an after-school program," once they have been underway for a while. But creating something new is really tough if you don't know where you are starting from or where you are at any given moment. That's why at inception and, in fact, everywhere along the route, entrepreneurs want to know what is. They want the clearest understanding of reality they can get. A key part of that understanding is knowing what resources they can draw on when getting underway.

With Prediction, you start with a goal and then create a plan to obtain it. Part of that plan is identifying and lining up the necessary resources. Only once this is done, do you act; that is, you don't take your first step until everything is in place.

People who excel at Creaction don't spend months or years assembling resources. They like to get started quickly—immediately, if possible. They also don't spend a lot of time planning and assembling

## It's Only Rock and Roll (but I Like It)

If you ever put on a play in your backyard or improvised a baseball diamond using a tree as first base and a lump of dirt as second, you instantly understand the concept of acting quickly with the resources at hand. (And you will recognize this story.)

Nia and Imani had been friends since elementary school. And friends being friends, they had a lot in common. Music was a huge part of both their lives.

Nia picked up the guitar in junior high and was a natural even though she was completely self-taught. Imani, who had ten years of piano lessons, loved singing and playing along with Nia, and their covers of rock songs and the few tunes they wrote on their own were pretty good—at least according to their friends who asked them to perform at parties.

Imani's brother went off to college and left her his rock organ, and the two women started adding it to what had become their show. It wasn't the big time, but they were getting booked and sometimes even paid for performing.

Luke liked listening to them. An accomplished guitar player and adequate singer, he filled out the sound, playing lead guitar and backing up the women on the vocals.

They still lacked drums, but the organ had a synthesizer, and Imani programmed drum tracks for it, which was better than nothing.

They had their own sound and performed only the music they liked. People started to get excited about them, and Caitlin (a drummer) found out about them and joined.

The Black Eyed Peas are not nervous. Yet.

But more important, for our purposes, this is the classic example of acting quickly with the means at hand.

resources. They begin with the means at hand, even if the means at hand seem to be nonexistent.

For example, a few years ago, Stever Robbins got excited about doing podcasts. He bought a little recorder and editing software but was never particularly successful. One day, acting on impulse, he wrote a letter to a popular podcaster he had never met, Grammar Girl, whose Web site he admired, and offered to do a business podcast for her. Out of sheer coincidence, she had just sold her podcast channel to Macmillan Publishers, which was looking for other podcasters to add to its stable.

A simple letter sent to someone he didn't know resulted in a new gig for Robbins. He now has 160,000 subscribers to his Get-It-Done Guy podcast and thousands of followers on Facebook and Twitter. The point? If you look around, you probably have more ways of getting started than you think. And who knows where it may lead?

---

The people who excel at Creaction don't spend months or years assembling resources. They like to get started quickly—immediately, if possible.

---

Where do you begin to take inventory of your resources at hand? We suggest you start with yourself and ask these three questions:

*Who am I?* What traits, tastes, skills, and inclinations do you have that you can draw on in starting a new venture?

*What do I know?* This includes your education, training, experience, and expertise.

*Who do I know?* Who can you draw upon right now—in your personal, social, and professional networks—to help this new idea succeed?

You can start your journey anywhere, of course. You might ask, "Where am I going to get the money to fund this thing?" "How can I get community support?" "Is now the time to relocate, before I set up shop?" But entrepreneurs like to get into action as soon as they can, and their own personal assets are immediately available. By asking the three questions, they are taking stock of the critical assets immediately at their disposal.

Because your personal assets are so important in getting started quickly and on firm footing, let's look at each in more detail.

## Who am I?

When you ask yourself "Who am I?" you are trying to find out what kind of a person you are, what kinds of things turn you on, what really matters to you, and what kind of things you will *not* do because either they go against your values or you just don't find them interesting enough to invest any time in. The answers give you a sense of self, which helps you to quickly eliminate ideas that don't fit. ("Hmm. This vague idea I have for finding smart, economically disadvantaged kids and steering them to the best possible colleges is appealing. But, you know, I also want to support myself. So as intriguing as the concept of a pro bono after-school program is, it won't provide me with a necessary income. I wonder what I can do that will get the result I want with the kids and give me a livable income?") You end up knowing what you want to do—and what you don't.

That is hugely important. As we've said before, the ability to focus your attention enables you to create with greater ease and consistency. You'll remember from chapter 2 (and from what you have experienced in your own life) that if you are distracted, disinterested, or dealing with something that doesn't excite you, it is hard to maintain focus. Creating under those conditions is extremely difficult.

We often are unaware of all our strengths . . . and weaknesses. Ask others to talk to you about what you are good at (and what you are not). You don't need to accept what they say as gospel, but they may find it easier to see things about you than you can.

Conversely, when you are in love with an idea, your attention takes care of itself. The big point here is that self-awareness is key. You need to know who you are and what you want. And what you don't.

## What do I know?

You never know where the insight that leads to an opportunity will come from. That is why the mental cataloging of what you know is important. For example, you may have gone to a school known for its rigor in math and the hard sciences. But it turns out that even though your degree is in engineering, you gain the most joy in your life by bringing together like-minded people. That's why, in thinking about what you know, you want to think about your personal and your professional lives. Again, you want to include everything you can possibly think of because at this point you simply can't decide what is going to be relevant.

## Who do I know?

The most successful entrepreneurs generally involve others in their new projects right from the conception of the idea. (We talk more about this in chapter 6.) They are looking to leverage their resources. (There is no reason to reinvent the wheel when a friend of a friend owns the world's biggest wheel store, or more concretely, you are thinking of starting a newsletter and Uncle Jim has a printing shop with idle capacity.)

What works for them should work for you, whether you are starting a business or trying to change an organization or forming a new club at your school. That's why determining who you know is so important. (See "Taking Inventory.")

## Taking Inventory

One of the best opening lines of any book is the first sentence of *Baby and Child Care* by Dr. Benjamin Spock: "You know more than you think you do."

That is true about parents; it's certainly true about anyone thinking about starting something new. As a way to help you think about what you truly know, break down the task by categories.

Ask, what you know:

- Professionally?

- From my training?

- Personally?

- About the world around me?

From there, you can ask:

- What aptitudes do I have? What am I good at?

- What did I learn in school that can help me?

- What have I learned from my personal and professional experiences?

And finally, you can move on to who you know. If you have ever planned a wedding or had to organize a huge party for all your friends and acquaintances, you are well aware that you know a lot more people than you think you do.

To help you generate a definitive list, you may want to start thinking of people you know by category, that is, you ask who you know:

- Personally?
- Socially?
- Professionally?

From there, you can add names by category, such as:

- People with money (if you need money for what you plan to do)
- People who want to take risks
- People who know other people
- People who would be fun to work with
- People who can get stuff done

Then you can sort by specific skills by asking (if you are starting a company) who do you know who knows a lot about:

- Finance?
- Marketing?
- Recruiting?
- Building a company?

Or if you are starting a new course at the local community college, who can:

- Get the word out?
- Help me double-check that I have covered everything I want to teach?
- Handle the paperwork?

We guarantee your answers to each question will trigger more than three potential ideas to pursue. (If they don't, keep asking.)

(For how these three questions work together, see "How This Plays Out in Real Life.")

## How This Plays Out in Real Life

Let's see how the three questions work together.

When Eliot Daley decided to leave his job as executive vice president of the production company of *Mr. Rogers' Neighborhood*, he had a lot of resources to draw on.

In answer to the "Who am I?" question, he could respond that he was a veteran of public television and someone whose personal interests included "tennis, sailing, golf, travel, theater, music, books, auto racing, fireworks, worship, kite flying, writing, singing, and daydreaming."

As for what he knew, the answer was "a lot." He had extensive experience raising funds from foundations, corporations, and government entities, and degrees in the social sciences and education and a bachelor's of divinity as well. And he had desire: "The common thread is my passion for working with others to envision, reach for, and achieve beneficial results for society."

The list of people he knew was extensive as well, given his business, personal, and educational background.

Capitalizing on everything he knew, Daley decided to "take an all-out plunge into the world of business by launching a new venture I had dreamed up myself. It was seemingly a can't-miss opportunity—great concept, and easy access to abundant funding, since going after funding for *Mr. Rogers' Neighborhood* was a big part of my job and I got to know this territory pretty well—especially the corporate and private sources.

"I was struck by two things: first, how relatively easy it was to get the dough, and second, how little thought the donors gave to their own strategy in the use of these precious dollars. For the most part, their grants seemed to be on-the-spot, up-or-down decisions in response to unsolicited proposals that came their way, rather than a decision designed to help fulfill a carefully wrought plan on their part to bring about a specified improvement in society. With few, if any, staff and during just a handful of casual meetings a year, the trustees would sift through the piles of incoming appeals, name their own favorites, distribute the money, have a nice lunch, and go home.

"To my entrepreneurial eye, this looked like a no-brainer: these foundations clearly need professionals to get them "on strategy," so I'll put together a Professional Foundation Staff for Rent—the first consulting group whose sole purpose is to help the trustees of these unstaffed private foundations plan and execute their philanthropic strategy. Brilliant!"

To find out how this "no brainer" played out, see chapter 5.

## Everything else

So you've made a good start in assessing your personal assets. What else makes up the means at hand? The short answer: anything that is both readily available and might be relevant. And you can instantly see the challenge. When you're operating in the unknown, it is impossible to know what is relevant or what might become relevant in the future. It is not always clear beforehand which pieces of information, or which potential assets, are worth paying attention to and which are not. This means everything is potentially important, at least initially. It is only later (or after the fact) that we know which things were critical and which were superfluous. Consequently, there is neither a theoretically right answer to this question nor a prescription for determining what might be a potential asset.

Making this harder, of course, is that whatever is relevant is going to depend on the situation. If you are starting a business, you want to know what is true about the technology that you might be employing or the market that you will be selling into. If you are trying to create a community recreation center, you probably want to know something about construction costs, traffic flows, and the interests of other members of your community. This is why you want to catalog every potential asset in figuring out your means at hand.

## Keep your eye on current reality

You've taken a realistic inventory of the potential assets around you. That's terrific, but you have to keep doing it. Updating your inventory doesn't happen automatically. You need to make it a habit. Not taking inventory can be problematic for two reasons.

First, you are likely to miss something important. A new asset. A new opportunity. A new discovery.

Second, by not working from an honest and current inventory of your assets, you are likely to make a flawed assumption. For example, you might assume it will be relatively easy to get the government to come along as a partner. "It will only cost each taxpayer $1.34," you say about a well-intentioned program you want to start, or you could contend that a new kind of wellness program "will pay for itself" (in reduced long-term health-care costs).

Both statements could be absolutely true, but when it comes to government spending, that is irrelevant. You need to know what politicians will and will not fund. Making assumptions based on nothing beyond what makes sense to you is not the right road to take.

If, on the other hand, you just assume the world is stuck in its ways, you could shortchange a potential opportunity, which of course is a central problem of Prediction. Coffee sales had been steadily declining for two decades before Howard Schultz created Starbucks. People assumed individuals wouldn't pay for television or radio before cable and SiriusXM came along.

In addition, if we aren't clear-headed about reality, we are likely to lapse into basing our actions on what reality was (not a good idea). You need to look no further than the American auto industry in the 1970s and 1980s ("Americans have always bought American cars and they always will").

When you are heading off into the unknown, understanding current reality is a very, very, very good idea.

## Just Start:
## An Exercise for Acting Quickly with the Means at Hand

1. Take one of the desires you were excited about from chapter 2.

2. Inventory all the things you have immediately and readily at hand. (The sidebar "Taking Inventory" earlier in the chapter can help.)

3. Determine the next step (any next step) you can take immediately toward your desire.

## Takeways

1. **Once you know what you want,** of course, you need to figure out how to get it. That means that right off the bat , you need to know what resources you have. You can find out by asking the questions: Who am I? What do I know? Who do I know?

2. **A key part of moving forward is understanding current reality.** The way the world really is is not necessarily the way you would like it to be. You might, indeed, be able to change the world. But

to do that, you need to understand where the world is now. This can be an Achilles' heel for entrepreneurs. They can get so caught up in what they are trying to do that they fail to perceive current reality as clearly as they might.

3. **Once you understand where you are and what resources are at your command,** you are prepared to take action, once you determine what you are willing to invest to "play." We turn to that question in the next chapter.

# 4

# Assess Your Acceptable Loss

Here's news that won't stop the presses: doing anything in the unknown entails risk. Given that, you need to decide how much you can afford to lose before you get underway. There is a way to keep those losses to a minimum and guarantee that if you fail, you fail quickly and cheaply while learning a lot. (And, after all, that is the second best outcome.) Here we show you how to minimize your potential losses.

THERE'S A REASON that seasoned entrepreneurs don't think of themselves as risk takers, even though everyone else does. They have developed terrific ways to limit potential losses as they start a new venture.

That fact surprises many people because if you read the popular press, you might well think that successful entrepreneurs love risk. Faced with the edge of a cliff, according to media accounts, they would prefer jumping off with a homemade parachute made of bedsheets to finding another way safely down.

That's simply not true. They like ropes and harnesses. More specifically, they prefer measured steps as they head off into the unknown and try to start their new venture. They don't like risk. They accept it as part of the game and then work extremely hard to reduce it to a minimum.

People who have started one or more ventures will tell you that you need to know how much you are willing to lose before you even begin to think about starting something new. And you need to do everything possible to make sure you don't exceed that figure.

Successful serial entrepreneurs adhere to the basic principles of risk management. If you're going to play in a game with uncertain outcomes: (1) don't pay or bet more than what you can expect as a return, and (2) don't pay or bet more than you can afford to lose.

Both of those ideas can be summed up with the phrase "acceptable loss," a concept in which you consider the potential downside of whatever risk you are about to take—such as starting a new company or some other venture that is going to consume a lot of your time, capital, or other assets—and put on the line no more than you find acceptable to lose should it not turn out the way you want.

This is, of course, not how risk is treated in the Prediction universe. In a predictable world, you spend a *lot* of time estimating the size of

## It's More Than a Math Problem

When you are thinking how much you should put at risk in starting a new venture, it's good to ask yourself, "How much can I afford to lose?" You might conclude that it is only an arithmetic problem: you want to make $100,000 on the venture. You want a four-to-one return. You are willing to risk $25,000. It all works out.

But while the math is right, it really doesn't take into account the desire driving your decision to create whatever it is you want to bring into being.

So, while mathematically a 4:1 return makes sense, you might in fact be willing to break even on your investment (or even lose money) if the idea is important enough to you. Hence the term acceptable loss, as in "don't lose more than what is acceptable to you," based on whatever calculus you use.

the prize—the financial rewards of pursuing a particular opportunity and optimizing the plan to achieve what those in the finance community call "the expected return." The logic is straightforward and looks something like this:

1. Analyze the prospective market and choose segments with the highest potential return.

2. Develop and optimize the plan for your product or service to achieve the expected potential.

3. Calculate the costs in money, time, and resources of achieving that potential.

4. Then discount whatever you came up with to account for the fact that nothing is certain.

This logic results in one number that tells you whether you should pursue the opportunity. If you work at a big company, this should sound very familiar. It's a logical result of years of conditioning to "maximize shareholder wealth."

---

The notion of investing substantial amounts of energy in calculating expected returns in a highly uncertain world is simply silly.

---

While it makes enormous sense in a predictable setting, this logic makes no sense at all in the face of the unknown. If you use this logic there, all you are doing is making projections on assumptions that are contingent on guesses, which you buttress with extensive studies and calculations. Finally, you pretend that you are creating certainty by multiplying the whole thing by something less than 100 percent to compensate for uncertainty in order to end up making seemingly rational decisions.

## Accounting Simplified

In addition to everything else, acceptable loss simplifies financing decisions. Here's why.

Business has all kinds of financial measures that help determine whether a potential new project is worth funding. An important one is "expected return," which can be defined this way: "How much money will we get back on each dollar that we invest?"

To calculate expected returns, we have to estimate future sales (uncertain) and potential market risks (uncertain), and then raise enough money not only to get underway but to hurdle all those (uncertain) obstacles your research uncovered. In contrast, to calculate acceptable loss, all we need to know is our current financial situation (known)—how much money and other assets we have in total (known)—and the absolute most we are willing to risk (or lose) (known). We commit to getting started with that amount of money, figure out a way to do it cheaper, or figure out a way to attract additional investors (something we will talk about in chapter 6.)

As you can see, the concept of acceptable loss transforms the decision-making process from juggling unknowns to working with knowns.

But the more uncertain the situation, the more this math is foolish. After all, there is little value in fine-tuning estimates of the unknown. And that explains why entrepreneurs and other creators use an opposite logic, that of acceptable loss. They don't spend much time forecasting or evaluating the comparative risks of the various opportunities they face. Instead of asking, "How big is it going be?" they ask, "Is it big enough to interest *me*?"

And instead of focusing on expected return, or how much they could possibly make, their attention is on acceptable loss, or how much they might lose, should things not turn out the way they hope.

## Limiting the downside is almost always good

As you can see, employing the concept of acceptable loss does two things: On the one hand, it keeps any failures small. By definition, you never lose more than you are willing to. On the other hand, it gives you a different way to evaluate an opportunity, a way that does not depend entirely on profits.

You entered into a new venture for some reason. It could be to make a lot of money, but it could be because of other reasons: "I can't stand my boss and I'm going off on my own." You might do it because of a noble aim: "I really want to help women back home," or it could just be that "if I don't start my own company now, I never will." Using acceptable loss frees you to use other motivations than generating the highest return on assets (although, as we said, "I want to make a lot of money" is a fine reason for starting a business).

But although the reason for starting a business can be open-ended, the amount of money at risk is clearly defined; it is limited by how much you find acceptable to lose.

---

If you want or desire to play in a game with uncertain outcomes:
1. Don't pay or bet more than what you can expect as a return, and
2. Don't pay or bet more than you can afford and are willing to lose.

---

How pivotal is the idea of acceptable loss? Of all the serial entrepreneurs Saras Sarasvathy studied, not one, before starting, "tried to garner specific information about potential returns or predict an ideal level of investment for their projects. Instead they wanted to spend only what they could afford to lose."

## It Works in Your Personal Life, Too

Our friend Heidi Guber reminds us that the concept of acceptable loss also works outside of work, in this good illustration of the concept of building off what you find (see chapter 5): "For a long time, on our anniversary, what my husband and I would do was search for the cheapest ticket we could find for any place in the world. The approach took us to the most wonderful places like Greece or Hong Kong, but we never knew where we were going until we found the best deal. As a result, we had these remarkable adventures we never could have planned."

And if things didn't work out, at least the vacation didn't cost very much.

## How acceptable loss works

As you prepare to take action, you need to ask two questions to make sure you stay within the bounds of your acceptable loss.

- What can I *afford* to pay to take the next step?

- What am I *willing* to pay to take the next step?

The costs we are talking about go beyond the financial. In fact, there are at least five classes of assets at your disposal and at risk.

1. **Money.** This is the most obvious, of course. Getting a new venture up and running can be costly, and you don't want it to be, if there is any way to help it.

2. **Time.** You want to guard your time just as much as you guard your money. And just as you have a dollar figure that you think would be "acceptable" to lose, you want to have a time limit as well. ("I am willing to give this idea up to six months to see if it will work.")

3. **Professional reputation.** We all have one, although when you are first starting out, it may be extremely slight. There is nothing wrong with failing if the idea you tried was worthy and you were sufficiently committed to it. You gave it your best shot. It didn't work, so move on to the next. But if you are seen as someone who doesn't anticipate obvious problems, or who can't conserve resources and use them properly, that failure can seriously hurt you in whatever you do next. You may find it far harder to raise money or even to get another opportunity. Damage to your professional reputation can be a huge loss.

4. **Personal reputation.** People may hate the question, "What do you do for a living?" arguing (correctly) that they are more than their job. Still, how people see you is partly shaped by how you earn your income. You don't want your new venture to be an embarrassment, which could affect your self-esteem or fail to represent who you truly are. This kind of loss is similar to a loss of professional reputation, but it hits literally much closer to home. Losing your standing with those near and dear to you, within your church, civic group, or whatever can be devastating. Unintelligent or frequent failures are embarrassing and carry psychosocial consequences.

   Moreover, one of the primary sources of resources for your venture comes from your family and friends, and you certainly don't want to waste their money (and your good graces), especially if it comes from your in-laws. And all the time you will be spending on the new venture will keep you away from kith and kin, so you want to choose whatever you plan to do extremely carefully to make that loss of spending time with them worthwhile.

5. **Missed opportunities.** If you are working to start venture X, you cannot be working on venture Y at exactly the same

moment, and Y could potentially be a far better idea. In business, this is known as an "opportunity cost"—the cost of *not* pursuing other opportunities. You want to be mindful of what you are choosing not to do and you also want to recognize other forms of opportunity cost: The price to be paid for not acting right away—someone else might conceive and implement your idea. And the price to be paid for inaction—you might spend the rest of your life in a job you hate or miss a great opportunity to make a once-in-a-lifetime contribution.

## The One That (Happily) Got Away

You can have a great idea and decide not to do anything with it, because you are convinced you can do something else even better. (The opportunity cost associated with your time is better spent elsewhere.) G. Michael Maddock, founder and CEO of Maddock Douglas, a leading innovation consultancy, explains:

> Speaking nonmetaphorically, I am a fisherman. Like most fishermen, I dream of coming up with the next great fishing lure. I carry around hundreds of different types of lures because I never want to be caught without the latest, greatest super bait. When it comes to fishing, I am always prepared, and I just assume every other former Boy Scout fisherman must behave the same way. Big market right?
>
> About ten years ago, on a freezing morning in the middle of Canada, I noticed an annoying challenge with jigs. [Note to non-fisherman: a jig is a simple, usually colored weight with a place to stick a hook in the back. You can add live bait or plastic worms to the jig—whatever you fancy.]
>
> Any fisherman who has used a jig has picked up one with the line hole, the place where you attach your hook, completely painted shut. The jigs are mass-produced and painted the same way, so it isn't surprising that that some would make their way into stores with the hole painted closed.

On that freezing cold morning in Canada I saw it as a huge problem waiting for an invention. And so the EyeOpener was born. This crafty little invention promised to save fishermen around the world hundreds of hours by popping the paint right out of the hole of the jig.

I talked about it and I talked about it. I took friends to coffee and asked if they thought it was a really big idea. I protected the name, I drew up the mechanicals, and then I didn't do a darn thing with it. Work, family, and other more promising ideas took precedence. It wasn't exactly that I had abandoned it. I would get around to it. Someday. It was a really good idea, but I had bigger fish to fry (so to speak).

I still remember my wife starting to cry in a Walmart in Iowa when she saw "my" idea being marketed by someone else. She had no idea that I had dozens of similar, even bigger "big ideas" in a drawer back home.

We doubt there is any reliable formula that can provide security when venturing into the unknown and make it more likely for a particular effort to succeed. But there is absolutely no doubt that Creaction will reduce the cost of failure, should there be one. If you fail, you fail cheaply.

## Money, Money, Money

The people who start successful companies time after time really do go into a venture thinking, "I can afford to lose X dollars on this and no more." But just because you can afford to lose $10,000 doesn't mean you want to. Obviously, you would prefer to lose far less—and presumably nothing—before getting underway.

However, action changes everything. You may go into the venture with $20,000 but believing you want to risk no more than

$10,000, but as you get underway, you might discover that just another $2,500 could put you over the top. All of a sudden, $12,500 becomes your acceptable loss figure.

Similarly, you could have said you would spend no more than three months determining if a new venture would work, but that might also change once you start.

This point is worth emphasizing, since it runs contrary to the image of entrepreneurs as people who constantly "swing for the fences," betting everything they own on new ventures. While that is sometimes true, most of the time, it's not. In general, they either prefer the cheapest alternative or come up with creative ways of doing things at little cost to themselves.

Furthermore, they explicitly see themselves as financially conservative. For example, one serial entrepreneur said, "When I start something, I am always aware of what I am spending. I always go the cheap route. I cover my costs so I don't have to take any huge risks if I can help it."

---

The concept of acceptable loss dovetails with two ideas we have already discussed. In asking "What can I afford to lose?" you are taking stock of your current reality. And by determining what you are willing (and prepared) to lose, you are double-checking your level of desire.

---

Not only are entrepreneurs fiscally prudent, they like the limitations that acceptable loss imposes. As Joshua Herzig-Marx, a founder of Incentive Targeting wrote on our blog, Action Trumps Everything, having a firm handle on your acceptable loss "is like walking into a casino with $50 in cash and no credit cards. Knowing how much you can lose, and trusting yourself not to exceed that amount, frees you to have more fun."

## Acceptable loss is extremely personal

Acceptable loss does not depend on the venture, but the individual. It varies from person to person, and across the course of someone's lifetime. (For example, you may be willing to risk more when you are young, knowing you will have decades to recover should things go wrong, less when your kids are approaching college age and you need to save every dollar you can for those upcoming tuition bills, and then more later once those bills are behind you.)

Let's see how acceptable loss plays out in practice. Consider the case of a man in his mid-forties who is thinking about quitting his high-paying job to start his own company. If our potential entrepreneur were to follow Prediction, he would do in-depth research to estimate not only the size of the market, but all the risks and challenges he might face (competitors, changing market conditions, and so on). The more potential risks or challenges he believed he was up against, the more money he would raise, in part to offset the uncertainty in his situation.

The potential entrepreneur might say, "I'd better do a business plan." (Months, maybe years pass while he does research and prepares the document.) At the end of that time, he says:

### The Worst That Could Happen

Postmortems, or trying to determine why an idea failed, are common in business. But wouldn't "pre-mortems," figuring out what could go wrong ahead of time, make more sense in business and any other place you are thinking of creating something new?

Here's how a pre-mortem could work. Before you start, assume the new venture you are about to undertake has failed spectacularly. Then write down every plausible reason you can think of to explain the failure. Then take steps to mitigate the potential problems.

A pre-mortem is a very useful exercise in reducing your risk.

It looks like I need $1 million to start my idea of creating a service that matches recent MBAs who have a scientific background with high-tech employers. Creating and maintaining the database is going to be a huge expense. Still my projections show this is the biggest potential market that matches my skill set. And they also show I'll break even in two years. I can put in $100,000, which is all the money I have saved and can get from family and friends. So, I need to raise another $900,000 before I can start. That's assuming that I'm okay giving up all the money I would have made at my day job for the next two years. Let me think about that over the weekend. [Some 72 hours later] Okay, I'm in. Let me start raising that $900,000.

In contrast, someone using Creaction would start by examining the means at hand, and what he can afford to lose. That leads to a very different interior monologue:

I am forty-six. I've always wanted to be my own boss. By drawing on my own resources and borrowing from family and friends, I have $100,000 I can commit to finally going off on my own. I need $50,000 for expenses and $50,000 to live on for the next six months until I get some revenue. In the worst case, the company I start goes under and I lose every dime. If that happens, I'm out the $100,000 and go back to my old job, or get a different job within the industry and figure out a way to pay back everyone I borrowed from. I am willing to risk that. If I end up losing the money, so be it. It won't be the end of the world.

But, if I don't take this risk now, when am I going to do it? I don't want to wake up twenty years from now and be one of those people who talk about "what might have been."

It's a sad thing to have regrets about something you wanted to do but never did. My family is onboard with me taking the risk, and while I know every new venture is a crapshoot, I feel pretty good about this. I am going to do it and adjust on the fly if I have to. My basic premise must be right. There is an unaddressed opportunity to serve the MBA market. I think the job-matching idea has a lot of promise, but if it turns out a Web site is better, or a newsletter or whatever, that's what I'll do, once I am underway.

Note, the person who is using Creaction is not thinking, "Where will I get the biggest bang for the buck?" or "What will lead to the most profit?" Instead, he is acting out of desire. This is something that he wants to do. He expects to be successful, but has identified his acceptable loss.

As you can see, acceptable loss frees you to focus on immediate options that generate more options for the future. This will only work, of course, if you are willing to adjust the shape of your venture ("I'll do something to serve the recently minted MBA market" as opposed to "I'm only interested in a job-matching service for recently minted MBAs with a technology background".) In other words, if you adapt to your means, rather than remaining fixated on one specific goal, you end up having more options to pursue.

## Starting with few resources

While managers are taught to analyze the market and choose target segments with the highest potential return, people starting a business using Creaction tend to find ways to reach the market with a minimum expenditure of resources such as time, effort, and money.

In the extreme case, it means starting a company with virtually no resources. That isn't hyperbole. Just think about all the technology companies—Hewlett-Packard and Apple among them—that began, at least metaphorically, in someone's garage.

And not only do they often start on the proverbial shoestring, serial entrepreneurs commonly do not do much traditional research before getting underway. Instead they often take a prototype to the nearest potential customer and, in an attempt to receive an order, describe in elaborate detail the ultimate features and benefits.

Why? You learn a lot by how those potential buyers react. You find out where the obstacles are, what questions customers and potential customers have, and what you could charge. You might even get some cash. So the market research is actual selling. And the fact is that *until someone buys your widget, the idea for creating a new company is imaginary.* Not until the first sale is it real.

## Winning by losing

The concept of acceptable loss can provide more opportunities to start new businesses for the simple reason that you are likely to get more times at bat in the same elapsed time. Why? First, there are lower costs to get underway, so you can start sooner. As opposed to Prediction, where you line up all your resources ahead of time, people who employ Creaction take small steps toward their goal. Often this means you get the market's "reality check" sooner. Second, because of lower costs, you can stay in the game longer and can rapidly adjust as you proceed. At any point in the journey, if you decide it isn't going to work, you quit. That also limits your loss. Both those elements mean that if you fail, you fail fast and cheaply. That frees up resources—both time and money—for you to try something else.

Even if you start a new venture and get to the end point—defined as reaching the limits of what you were prepared to lose—the decision to quit (either because you no longer have the desire to continue or the market isn't interested in what you have) isn't fatal, since you didn't risk more than you could afford. It is simply time to regroup and think about what you want to do next.

Contrast that to what happens if you employ Prediction. You seemingly plan forever. You assemble a team, which takes more time. If you go the traditional funding route and look for venture capital money, it can take as long as two years (really) to get the money you need, if venture capitalists decide to fund you, and they probably won't. They fund about 1,200 of the 600,000 new businesses started every year. Of those 600,000, the U.S. Small Business Administration says 66 percent survive two years, and other research shows 44 percent survive eight years.

If you do the math, you'll find that in the same two years, you might start and fail in two ventures and begin a third. The odds favor one of them working, and you would have a good chance of owning 100 percent of a successful firm, as contrasted with a 0.2 percent chance of owning a venture capitalist–funded firm.

---

In the worst of all possible worlds, you are going to fail quickly and cheaply as a result of using Creaction. That is not a bad thing.

---

And remember, while you are spending all this time finding someone to give you the money, the marketplace is changing, and by the time you get funding, your window of opportunity may have closed.

## Acceptable Loss and Capital-Intensive Industries

Here's a question we're asked a lot: "But what if I need $250 million [or some other huge number] to get my venture off the ground? Does the concept of acceptable loss work here as well?"

The short answer is: "Sort of."

The longer answer is: "Not really." (And that's not a bad thing.)

Let us explain both answers.

Clearly, you can use all the principles of acceptable loss to help you determine if you are truly committed to starting your manufacturing facility, biotech lab, or whatever the venture is that will consume a lot of capital. But at some point, you are going to need to attract serious money to make it happen. And that will mean finding serious investors, investors who are going to rely—and will want you to rely—on Prediction.

That's perfectly fine. Remember what we have said from the beginning. Creaction—and acceptable loss is part of Creaction—isn't designed to replace Prediction. There are still going to be places—such as raising huge amounts of capital—where Prediction, with its emphasis on future cash flows and return on investment, will and should dominate. This is one of those places, so predict away.

One more thing about this. Those investors you are seeking huge bucks from are going to look into your background to see if you have ever started another successful venture. As we have discussed, the fastest way to get a new venture up and going is by using Creaction. So if you don't have a success under your belt, you may want to use Creaction to help you gain one (or two) before you go searching for the big bucks.

## Getting started quickly

In chapter 3, we said that entrepreneurs like to get started quickly with the means at hand. Now we can return to how they can start quickly. It's really pretty simple: *when you want something and your next step is within your means and within your acceptable loss, the most natural thing in the world is to act.* Under these circumstances, it is really unnatural not to act.

This is the secret of seasoned entrepreneurs and why they *seem* so impulsive. They drive the cost of their next step down to the point where it makes no sense not to act, given that they imagine accomplishing something they want. They construct and play a game in which no one decision is likely to be fatal and where moving quickly and correcting mistakes as you go along are more intelligent than overthinking.

The recipe for acting quickly is really pretty simple: make sure that this is something that you want and get creative to devise an acceptably inexpensive next step with the means immediately available to you. If you do these things, the next thing you will find is that you are taking action.

## *Just Start:*
## An Exercise for Assessing Your Acceptable Loss

When it comes to determining how much you can personally risk in starting a new venture, that is, your own acceptable loss, ask yourself these questions:

- What are my assets?
- What can I afford to lose?
- What am I willing to lose in the worst case?

With that by way of context, think about the step you imagined taking at the end of chapter 3. Is it within your acceptable loss?

Explain to a friend what your desire is and the next step you imagine taking. Work together to reduce the cost (money, time, reputational capital, and so on) even further.

Now, if you wish, you can take the step.

## Takeaways

1. **Know how much you are willing to risk before getting underway.**

2. **Try to not lose much (or anything at all).** Your goal, of course, is spend as close to zero as you can.

3. **Walk away if you discover you no longer want it** or when you become convinced that you cannot succeed for technical, market, or personal reasons (such as exceeding your acceptable loss).

# 5

# Build on What You Find

As we have seen professional creators—such as entrepreneurs and anyone else who brings something into being that has never existed before—like to know how things really are. That's especially true when they encounter problems and surprises. They also believe, counterintuitively, that if something goes wrong, it is a good thing—potentially a very good thing. They believe problems and obstacles are actually assets. Let's see why.

WE KNOW. Saying "there are no such things as problems, just opportunities," sounds like a cliché. But the fact is:

- Creaction is based, in part, on that assertion. And

- Entrepreneurs invariably point to it as one of the reasons for their success.

In the Prediction world we grew up in, we were taught either to avoid the unexpected or to overcome it. It's all about efficiency. Optimizing. Achieving the objective quickly with as few deviations as possible. That makes a lot of sense in the Prediction universe. Once you have spent all this time figuring out what you should want and planning how to get it (predicting), then it's all about making that prediction a reality. So, not surprisingly, people get upset when something unexpected (and presumably unwanted) appears in their path. Any deviation needs to be eliminated or overcome as quickly as possible.

However, Creaction is all about exploiting the contingencies and leveraging the uncertainty by treating unexpected events as an opportunity. Those who are successful in starting companies, or creating anything new for that matter, learn not only to work with the surprise factor but also to take advantage of it.

Because people who use Creaction often begin with a relatively loose notion of their goals ("I want to find a job in the entertainment industry"), they can incorporate what they learn from the problems or obstacles they encounter along the way. ("Hmm. I thought there would be a chance to open my own nightclub that could feature cutting-edge bands. But that market is already sewn up in the place where I want to live. That's just the reality I face. Maybe I can either figure out a way to work with those clubs—I could serve as a talent scout—or take advantage of the work they have already done. I could create a Web site devoted to the new music scene and get the clubs to advertise.")

## Another Reason This All Sounds Familiar

Incorporating the obstacles or opportunities in our path is how most of us stumbled into our careers. While there were some people who knew they were going to be firefighters, doctors, or accountants from an early age, the rest of us took an entry-level job in a field we (sort of) liked, and our careers evolved from there. If you ask people in their fifties if they could ever have imagined back in high school that this is the way they would be earning their living, we bet you that 85 percent of them would say, "Heck, no."

In executing most plans, surprises are bad. But people who employ Creaction do not tie themselves to any theorized or preconceived market, strategic universe, or set path for making their idea a reality. For them, problems are a potential resource as opposed to a disadvantage. ("Who knew I would end up starting a Web site supported by the very clubs that I thought would be my competitors?")

---

Problems are good news (almost always).
Really.

---

They very often do something with the things that surprise them, treating those surprises as a gift (see the section on "Bad News" later in the chapter). Let's spend a couple of minutes trying to understand why that is true and learn why obstacles can be a good thing.

## How the world works

As we have said from the beginning, in the face of the unknown, action trumps everything, including thinking. One of the key reasons it does is that you never know for sure your thinking or planning is correct until you take action to discover if you are right. You may believe you know how the market will react, or whether you can find a customer for your product, or people who will support your new nonprofit idea, but until you actually do something to find out, you'll never know for sure.

But what this means is that every step you take in the journey could change where you decide to end up.

---

You are only one thought away from an insight that can make a problem go away, perhaps turning it into an opportunity in the process.

---

Here's why. Every action you take causes a change in reality. (Thinking doesn't.) You thought you would be able to sell one hundred widgets a day, but it turns out the market reacted by buying two hundred (or fifty). You then have to stop and reflect on the results of your action and see what you have learned from selling more (or less) than you expected. You are no longer speculating about what might happen. You know. Now you have to figure out what it means and what you are going to do next.

How do you get creative with a surprise? Well, if the surprise is a good one, you take full advantage of it. For example, you thought everyone in the world would love your new iPhone accessory. They did, but now you are overwhelmed by demand.

## To Help Your Thinking

Place a piece of 8.5" x 11" paper sideways and write what you want to create at the top.

Divide the paper into thirds with two vertical lines.

In the left column, list the problem(s) or obstacle(s) you are facing, things that are keeping you from achieving what you desire. It can be one thing or many.

Then spend five minutes figuring out as many ways as possible to solve these problems and write those solutions in the middle column.

When you are done, show your list of problems (and potential solutions) to someone else and have him or her help build on your solutions.

Once that is done, take a different tack with the left column. Instead of trying to solve those problems, assume they can't ever be solved, and take five minutes with your friend and figure out how that situation might become an asset or an unrecognized opportunity. Put these assets in the right column.

What convinced us that this exercise is fun is that even a cartoon antihero, Homer Simpson, can do it.

After realizing he has lived half his life and doesn't have much to show for it, Homer is inspired by Thomas Edison and sets out to become a successful inventor. Not surprisingly, given that this is Homer, most of his inventions—a horn that sounds every three seconds when things are fine; a gun that women have to aim at their face to apply makeup—are profoundly silly.

But in the midst of creating these dumb ideas, Homer inadvertently comes up with a good one.

As part of his thinking process, Homer invariably leans back in his chair . . . and promptly falls over. This happens repeatedly. To solve the problem, he creates a chair with two hinged legs on the back, making it impossible to tip over backward.

If Homer can turn a problem into an innovative solution, you have to believe we all can.

The logical thing to do is to ramp up production, add distributors (perhaps worldwide), maybe raise prices, and think about creating additional products not only for the iPhone but for all other smartphones, like BlackBerrys. You might pursue this path for the rest of your life, or until it no longer feels right (it is taking up too much time; you realize you never wanted to run a company, only start one.) At that point, you might sell what you have and do something else. Companies morph all the time, sometimes to great success. The Marriott hotel chain began life as a nine-stool A&W Root Beer stand. The extremely fashionable and upscale store Barney's in New York began as a discounter that sold showroom samples, retail overstocks, and manufacturers' closeouts bought at auctions and bankruptcy sales.

If the surprise was a negative one—that is, your actions did not go as you thought they would; you encountered a problem or even a setback— it is then time to figure out a way of using that negative to your benefit.

---

Problems and even setbacks are resources to employ to your advantage.

---

Let's say that the way your product attached to the phone unexpectedly interfered with the transmission characteristics of the antenna. Users complained of more dropped calls. You figured out how to change the design to negate this and in the process ended up with a product that not only worked much better, but looked a lot cooler. Even better, a year later when a major manufacturer tried to imitate your product, it made the same mistake that you had originally made and got egg all over its face. Suddenly you are the only company to turn to for a cool-looking phone that can actually make and receive calls.

## Problems = Advantage

Running headlong into a problem and then solving it can give you a barrier to competition, or at least a remarkable head start in the marketplace. Why? Because you acted, and the competition didn't. As a result, you know something they don't.

When Isadore Sharp, founder of the extremely upscale Four Seasons Hotels and Resorts, started out, he assumed that the only thing that would matter for him was to be in the best locations. The problem he ran into was that every other hotel chain had the same idea. That was a huge negative surprise. If you are doing what everyone else is, you don't have an advantage.

In solving that problem, Sharp stumbled on what turned out to be the Four Seasons' ultimate competitive advantage. He created a two-pronged barrier to entry, as he explains in his autobiography, *Four Seasons: The Story of a Business Philosophy*: "One was our inventory of hotels . . . the largest group of authentically first-class hotels in the world, a physical product no other company had to the same degree." The advantage was that he could offer the frequent traveler luxury one-stop shopping when staying in any of the world's major cities.

The other advantage was his people: "Three decades ago, we had decided that what our customers most desired was whatever would make time away from home most pleasurable and productive. So, we set about raising service levels to match our first-class decor, a historic judgment call that had made superior service the major determinant of hotel profitability and competitiveness, and while finally recognized now by every hotel company in the world, we had a long head start."

According to Sharp, "Location was no longer foremost in getting and keeping customers, it was people, people, people. This was now the decisive factor in our two-fold barrier to entry."

As we said, a negative surprise that you encounter can ultimately become a barrier to competition, if you treat it like a gift as Sharp did. He accepted the problem that what he thought was going to be an advantage—location—wasn't. (Everyone else could build in the same place.) He then took that fact (he had terrific locations, but many other people did, too) and asked what he could do with that. His conclusion: we can provide excellent service at these superior locations. That has given him a terrific edge in the marketplace.

## Obstacles welcome

Everything is a gift. Well, maybe not every single thing imaginable, but assuming that everything is a gift is a good way of looking at the problems or surprises you'll encounter in getting a new venture off the ground.

Why should you react to a problem with gratitude, whether you are trying to start a business or create something else? There are a number of reasons. First, you were going to find out eventually what people did and did not like about your idea. Better to learn it and learn it *now* before you sink more resources into the venture.

And as we have discussed, that feedback could help you take your product or service in another direction, or serve as a barrier to your competitors.

## From No-Brainer to Disaster to a New Idea

Remember Eliot Daley from chapter 3?

A veteran of working with Fred Rogers, of *Mr. Rogers' Neighborhood*, Daley was convinced he had spotted a huge opportunity: supplying professional support services to the nation's thousands of small, private foundations, most of which operated on an extremely ad hoc and informal basis.

In picking up the story; he told us:

Before I leapt, I thought it might be wise to consult with someone who knew the territory. Robert Goheen had recently followed up his distinguished tenure as president of Princeton University with a new job as head of the Council on Foundations, a philanthropic "trade group." I called on him and described my concept. "Forget about it," he said.

Well, *that* was hardly the advice or encouragement I was looking for. Beg your pardon, Dr. Goheen?

"These people are very self-satisfied," he explained. "All they want are congratulations, plaques, and dinners in their honor. And their names on buildings."

But, what about repairing their apparent lack of strategy, about increasing their efficacy, about helping them—in words of one syllable—get more bang for the buck?

"They don't care about that," he replied. "Look, it's very easy to seem successful at this game. The IRS says that you must distribute to qualified 501(c)(3) nonprofit organizations an amount equal to 5 percent of your assets or equal to all of your investment income—whichever is greater—minus reasonable administrative expenses. How hard can that be?"

Convinced the Goheen was wrong, Daley hired staff and started to go on sales calls and nothing happened. Actually, it was worse than nothing. Everyone he met with was pleasant, promised to think seriously about his idea, and then never made a decision to go ahead.

Eventually, he realized the small foundations were happy working the way they were. Random and ad hoc suited them fine. Goheen had been right.

What Daley needed was to sell the idea to places where there was—or should be—accountability for charitable giving. Framed that way, he knew who to go after: the nation's corporations.

Daley recalls,

Once the concept was clearly nailed down, I set out to bag a flagship client. I decided to start at the top with what was at that time the largest corporation in America—AT&T, which had nearly a million employees and a near-total monopoly in the telephone business in the U.S. I approached Charlie Brown, then the chairman and CEO of AT&T, a friend who I knew from our small tennis club in Princeton, and Charlie introduced me to Ed—the senior executive who was responsible for AT&T's massive advertising, public relations, and corporate contributions programs. Ed and I arranged to meet for lunch at his club in New York City.

The waiter took our drink order and Ed got right down to business. "Okay, Eliot, you called this meeting. What's on your mind?"

"As I understand it, Ed, you're responsible for advertising, PR, and corporate contributions at AT&T, right?" I responded.

"Yep."

"Well," I continued, "you have an outside agency that handles your advertising—N.W. Ayer, right?"

"Yep. Been together for almost a hundred years. We like long relationships."

"And you have an outside agency that handles AT&T's PR, too."

"Right. It's also a longtime relationship. Great people," Ed replied.

"Good," I responded and moved in for the coup de grâce. "We want to be your outside agency for corporate contributions."

Ripples of puzzlement danced fleetingly across Ed's face as he slowly tipped his head forward so far I couldn't read his face anymore. A long moment later, he looked up, fixed me with a clear eye, and said firmly, "Okay, you're hired."

It really was that simple. Oh, there were a series of meetings with other people at AT&T over the next few months, but basically we had the go-ahead at that lunch.

And once Daley had AT&T as a client, he found it relatively easy to sign up other corporations as well.

The same holds true if you were surprised. Why were you surprised? By definition, you were probably predicting or expecting something else. Good for you! You acted and got evidence. True, it was not what you were expecting or even wanted, but, as we have pointed out, that still puts you ahead of the people who are employing Prediction. They are still predicting, and not acting. Thus, they don't have evidence. All they have is what they think may be true. In contrast, you know something they don't (yet), and that is an asset. How big a one is yet to be seen.

## Bad news

Okay, so it's not a surprise. It's a disappointment—so bad that no reasonable person can define what you've encountered as anything but a problem. Most people will try to solve it and get rid of it. That's fine if you can. The problem has gone away, and, again, you've learned something that others might not know.

Ron Sarni and Todd Saunders know all about surprises big and little. They were convinced they had spotted a huge opportunity: they would create a fleet of food trucks that would serve Boston. There was only one problem, as Sarni explained: "We quickly found out that food trucks were banned in Boston. I mean they were illegal. You couldn't have them. And so our first order of business was to actually change the hearts and minds of city officials."

Surprisingly, they did. And the key, not surprisingly, was understanding politics. Food trucks appeal to people aged eighteen to thirty-four. And who comprised the biggest voting bloc supporting Boston City Council President Michael Ross? People eighteen to thirty-four.

But government being government, there were conditions that came with the go-ahead. One was that every food truck had to offer at least one "healthy option" on its menu. People who subsequently joined with Sarni and Saunders to create a food truck association complained this seemed to be "Big Brotherism," but Sarni got them to see the mandate differently: "What a gift. They were serving as our focus group. Bureaucracy runs by public opinion. So if they're telling us that we need a healthy food item, well, they were a built-in focus group telling us what the public really wants."

But what if you can't solve the problems you face. Try this: accept the situation to the point of embracing it. Take as a given that it won't ever change and turn it into an asset. What can you do with the "fact" that it won't ever change? Maybe it presents a heretofore unseen opportunity. Maybe you build it into your product or service in a way that no competitor (having not acted) could imagine. Instead of resisting and lamenting it, treat it as a gift and turn it to your advantage, something that the competition won't have, something that will serve as a protectable barrier to entry, if only for a while.

You see this all the time. People with a health problem (diabetes, for example) start services to help those who are afflicted. Yvon Chouinard, an avid rock climber, couldn't find equipment he liked, so he created his own. You probably know him better as the founder of Patagonia. Bernie Goldhirsh struggled for years trying to start a sailing magazine in the early 1970s. His problem? There were no resources for budding entrepreneurs to draw on. And so he started *Inc.* magazine to help people just like him.

The thing to remember is this: in the unknown, effective people work with what they have at hand—whatever comes along. They try to use everything at their disposal. That is why they are grateful for surprises, obstacles, and even disappointments. It gives them more information and resources to draw upon.

Another thing to remember: the lower your mood, the less likely you are to see reality clearly. So the state of disappointment makes it more likely that you will miss an opportunity right in front of you. Yes, you are upset. Get over it! Embrace reality and start embracing your gifts.

## Coming full circle

The message of this chapter is pretty simple. If you come across lemons—otherwise known as business problems or obstacles—do indeed make lemonade.

Try this approach next time you encounter something unexpected. Despite how unpleasant it seems, say, "This is really good news," and then try to make it so. The heart of Creaction is the ability to turn the unexpected to your advantage. That means your default position should be that there is never a problem without a potential profitable or pleasant solution lurking somewhere.

Let's return to the thread we launched at the beginning of chapter 3. Understanding exactly the situation you face, problems and all, reestablishes creative tension. This tension exists whenever there is a gap between what you've got and what you want. That gap fuels invention and action in favor of your desires.

The desire part is relatively easy. You can't escape what you want. Clarity about reality is the challenge. You always want to know the truth about where you are, and no matter how bad it may seem, you want to know what is real. The most straightforward way of doing that is to accept reality. Make it your friend. If you're disappointed, move on anyway. Nothing quite eradicates a bad mood as quickly or as well as making progress on something that you care about.

## *Just Start:*
## An Exercise for Turning Liabilities into Assets

Finding solutions to the problems that you encounter or to the things that have you stuck can be difficult. One reason it is so hard is because you are the person trying to solve the challenge at hand. You see things a certain way. And the flaw with that, as Einstein is said to have observed, is "problems cannot be solved by the same level of thinking that created them."

To escape that difficulty, sit down with someone, describe your problem, and then say to the person you're with, "Tell me five ways this could be an asset for me."

If you do—and listen with an open mind to what the person has to say—three things might happen, all of them good:

- Simply explaining the problem aloud could give you an insight into solving it.

- Your friend might actually come up with a solution.

- Even if she doesn't, her suggestions could spark new thinking on your part.

## Takeaways

1. **If you are faced with a pleasant surprise,** for example, more people liked your idea than you could have ever imagined, simply proceed down the path you were heading—although you might want to move a bit faster to make sure the opportunity window doesn't close.

2. **If the surprise is unwanted,** treat it as a gift and accept it wholeheartedly. It gives you new information, new evidence, that your competition does not have. Solve it, if you can. If you can't, see if it points to an opportunity or make it an asset (and build it into your product).

3. **Attitude is key.** If you assume that everything, even the unexpected, is a gift, it almost invariably will be.

# 6

# Bring Other People Along

Having a large pool of people who can help make your vision come true is a wonderful resource. That's why you want to view everyone as a potential customer or collaborator. How can you enroll people in your idea and what can you do with them once you have them onboard? Let's see.

PEOPLE WHO WANT TO DISMISS Creaction out of hand, for whatever reason, tend to say: "This is nothing more than ready, aim, fire." But the real summary is: "Aim. Fire." There's not a lot of getting ready.

What we have been saying in the first five chapters is that when you are in a situation where you don't know what is going to happen next, and the cost of acting to find out is low, then fire with what you have at hand or what you can assemble quickly.

We have seen that serial entrepreneurs usually don't spend a lot of time doing traditional research. They prefer to discover if there is a market or audience for what they want to do by going out and asking people if they want to buy. That's the only way to know for sure and it is consistent with their desire to be grounded in reality.

Serial entrepreneurs certainly don't do a lot of competitive analysis. In one study, some 74 percent reported they are not concerned with competitors, or that they consider potential competitors irrelevant until they know if there is a market for their idea.

But one place where they say they spend a lot of time—and they urge you too as well, whether you are starting a new company or anything else—is in trying to get as many committed people as they can to enroll in their efforts early on. Having self-selected, committed stakeholders join you is a way to spread the risk, confirm that you have a worthwhile idea, obtain additional resources, and have more fun. Serial entrepreneurs told Saras Sarasvathy that they believed that the growth of their potential enterprise was limited only by the number of collaborators they could attract, not by how much money they could raise.

Because bringing others along is such a big idea, it is worth spending some time exploring it. First, we'll put what we are discussing next in context. Then we'll give you a proven approach so that you can enroll others yourself.

## The Advantages of Bringing Along Other Committed People

Intuitively, the idea of attracting other people to your cause makes sense, but let us list the specific advantages.

1. **You gain more resources to draw on.** Not only do you have more people to work with, those people have resources of their own that they can contribute to the effort.

2. **You spread the risk.** If other people are contributing their resources, you need to put in less of your own.

3. **There's more creativity.** Your mother was right. Two heads (or 43 or 167) are better than one when it comes to attacking the challenge you face.

4. **You have confirmation that you are onto something.** People would not be joining you unless they thought you had a potentially worthwhile idea.

## Tangible exchanges

If you're starting a business, the thing you want most is sales. Entrepreneurs passionately believe that. They start selling as soon as they can. Maybe they have a prototype. Maybe it's only a specification sheet. They simply don't wait for a polished product unless they have to.

---

Instead of worrying about being attacked from the outside by competitors, people who employ Creaction try to strengthen their base. One way to do that? Attract committed stakeholders who share your values and can build on and help you refine your vision.

---

This is still good advice even if you're not starting a business. If you have a new idea for a community center, for example, you'll want to find out if you have support, before you invest too much time and effort (and ideally those people will join in your effort.) Getting into the market early (to see if there is a "buyer" for your idea or someone who shares your desire) lowers your cost and spreads the risk. Moreover, having potential buyers (a consumer or partner) tells you that they like your idea and confirms that you're on a good track. It builds your confidence and credibility with others, which is an asset we discussed in chapter 5. When you are thinking of starting something new, you want to do an inventory of your assets. Attracting self-committed stakeholders clearly falls into the "who do I know" category; it is another way of expanding the means you have at your disposal.

Many of us have aspirations that exceed the assets we have at hand. By adding self-committed stakeholders, you are accumulating additional resources. The knowledge network and assets these people have can be added to your own. That's no small thing, since very few of us

> ## Teamwork
>
> Many entrepreneurs and experts shared with us the observations that "investors bet on jockeys, not horses" and "ideas are a dime a dozen." For many, the team is more important than the idea, and investors, particularly early-stage ones, place more stock in the quality of the team than in any particular idea. The team becomes more important than a supposedly good idea, simply because ideas change so much during development.
>
> Contrary to popular wisdom, many great companies are founded by a great team coming together in advance of a particular idea.

have the wherewithal and/or abilities to start something completely from scratch.

Of course, some people prefer to go it alone. A friend of ours in the construction business started as a framer and bootstrapped himself to the point where he is now constantly building six new homes at a time. He is worth millions, and he owns 100 percent of his business. He took an extremely long time to get to this point, because he financed everything himself. He was willing to take 100 percent of the risk in exchange for 100 percent of the gains. But he is not most people. The vast majority of successful entrepreneurs we know bring others into the process early on. Babson College research shows there are fewer and fewer examples of entrepreneurs going it alone.

## Co-creation

The committed stakeholders who join you will help change your original idea, if you bring them in early enough in the process. They end up being collaborators and taking ownership of what is created. They become, in the very real sense of the word, co-creators. The initial vision becomes shared, it expands, and it becomes "ours" instead of just yours.

As you scale up, you will bargain and negotiate with the people who join (this is not a bad thing; they are smart and have good ideas), and as a result move from "me" to "we." As in, "we want to do this going forward" instead of "this is what I want to do."

Because of this addition, the process you will go through in creating something new will look like this. As you get these committed stakeholders—these are people who have actually invested money or other resources; they are not those who have only graced you with their advice and opinions—to join, you should take their input and suggestions into account without regard to *possible* stakeholders who may or may not join later. In other words, the people who are there today determine the course of the venture. It's likely that some people will come along later, and your product, service, or idea will be less appealing to them because of the actions you have already taken and so they will not want to join. So be it. You are operating in the here and now.

## Customers Can Be Co-Creators, Too

Although most of us don't think of them this way, customers end up shaping our ideas. They can ask for new features ("is it possible to make it sync with my laptop?") or features (you know I would love to buy it, if it only had a Y"). But ultimately you are the one who gets to decide if incorporating those ideas is a good thing.

For example, Melinda, who has taken a few years out of her career to raise her family, meets Jeff, an American Home Goods senior vice president, at a barbeque. Jeff has recently gotten interested in analytics, the emerging field that, among other things, measures the return on investment on advertising expenditures.

Melinda says, "Jeff, as part of my master's work, I built a simple scanner that tracks eye movements. I can tell to the nanosecond how much time someone spends reading a message—like an ad—how much attention they pay to each word and phrase. If I built you one for evaluation, would you buy it?"

Jeff says, "Sure," and he offers to put one of his company's best technical people on the project. Melinda contacts her old lab partner, Matt, and a week later they appear with their prototype. Jeff is simply thrilled and buys ten of them for further testing by all marketing divisions of the company, with the promise to buy a hundred more, if things work out. A few weeks later, Melinda delivers the test units, and while she's there, she asks Jeff for the names of others who might be interested. Jeff refers her to Mal and Denise.

Mal loves it, too, but for his purposes, the scanner needs to be able to connect to a PC via a USB to make field studies easier. Confident that she and Matt can provide that, Melinda takes Mal's order for twenty.

Denise loves it too, but needs to measure respiration and heart rates as well (as a way to measure the emotional impact of the ads).

"That will just require us to add existing monitors. Easily done," says Melinda, who takes an order for another twenty. Denise has a small pilot production shop with idle capacity, and she and Melinda work out a deal for Denise to get her enhanced twenty units in exchange for producing the other units Melinda needs for her other customers. Mal and Denise each give Melinda more referrals at the same time.

And the process continues. Not everyone buys, of course. Melinda takes orders from the customers who like it the way it is. Others request an additional feature, and if Melinda believes she can and wants to add that feature, she takes their order. Or she turns it down if it is technically or financially infeasible or represents too big a diversion or distraction from her vision. Still others say that if it had a certain feature, they'd consider it. Melinda is grateful for what she learned from these folks, but generally ignores people who don't give an order.

It's not too long before Melinda and Matt have given birth to a line of four "biometric" products. Sales are soaring.

Of course, the people who are involved with you employ their own understanding of acceptable loss to decide how much they are willing to risk in your venture. You need to keep that in mind. While it is certainly possible that they will contribute significant amounts of assets (money, time, contacts) to your venture, the odds are that their investment will be far less than yours. Like you, they are going to contribute according to what they want and can afford, and your venture may not be the most important thing going on in their lives.

---

Interactions with other people who make commitments yield new means and, in many cases, new goals. This process iterates as you keep adding self-selected stakeholders and continues until you reach the point where the new customer's requirement would stretch your product too far, either technically, financially, or you simply don't want to make any more changes.

---

Can there be a problem with involving too many stakeholders? Absolutely. If they are the ones with the money, they could try to take you in a different direction than you want to go ("I know you want to do X, but I am only going to provide the money if you modify X"). All those competing voices, ideas, and personalities can make moving forward a whole lot like herding cats. Either you learn to manage this situation—there are entire books on the subject—or you decide to do something else.

## Getting the most out of stakeholders

To make sure you achieve the maximum benefit of adding committed stakeholders, remember that:

- **Everyone should be focused on current reality.** Your immediate goal should be taking the next smart step toward what you want to accomplish and not focusing on what could happen.

- **Everyone is a potential stakeholder until proven otherwise** (by saying no), but only people who commit get a say in shaping the outcome. Others just get to express an opinion.

- **Everyone commits only to what he or she wants and can afford to lose,** not what is calculated to reach goals. If someone has committed $1,000 to help you, but you need $5,000, don't browbeat him into providing the additional $4,000. Find it elsewhere. Acceptable loss for others is different than it is for you. Acknowledge that and move on.

- **As more commitments are made,** goals become constrained and solidified to the eventual point that new members must more or less take it as they find it. At some point, it becomes too late to dramatically alter the product, service, or idea being considered.

## Intangible exchanges

By now the idea of obtaining additional self-selected, committed stakeholders probably appeals to you, so let's turn our attention to how you gain the commitment of others. For this, we need to look at something that, while related and often commingled and confused with selling, is quite different. We're talking about enrollment.

Enrollment is *not* about getting somebody to do something that you want them to do. It's about offering them the chance to do something they might want to do (in this case, becoming part of your effort). You don't convince them. They truly convince themselves. So, it's about enabling them to put their own name on the roll of the people who are going to be involved with you. It's generally to your advantage to have as many people committed to (enrolled in) your project as possible, even if none of them are prospective buyers or users of what you want to create.

How you get that enrollment to happen is a pretty straightforward process.

## Where do you begin? Step 1. Be enrolled yourself

You can't expect to gain the commitment of others if you're not committed yourself. You must *want* to make your idea a reality. Starting anything new is hard enough if you are committed. If you are not, you raise the degree of difficulty exponentially. Others can sense if you are not enrolled. They can tell you are not excited about the idea or truly committed to making it happen. And if they get that feeling, they are bound to ask, "If she is not really into it, why should I be?"

If you try to enroll someone when you are not truly enrolled yourself, you end up selling, and you probably won't even do a very good job of it. As we will see, selling and enrollment are different things.

## Step 2. Honesty

Okay, you are truly committed to the idea. Now you want to get people to come along. What's the next step? You talk to anyone and everyone about what you want to do. And you are genuine and transparent. You give them a complete picture. Not only do you tell them the positives and negatives, to the extent you know them, you also tell them why your idea is so important to you. If it is because you want to make a lot of money, tell them. If it really is all about making a small part of the world a better place, say that. Remember, one of the results in enrolling people is a lasting relationship. You do all of this because you want first and foremost an authentic relationship on which to build trust and joint action. You can only build this kind of meaningful relationship if you are being forthright.

What you are hoping for is that people will enroll with you and be inspired to take action. One of the first actions you want them to take is to tell you what they think of your idea. If you're sitting there talking to someone about what is really important to you, it is natural to want to know if what you are excited about rings his chimes; you want to know if it did anything for him. You want to hear something back!

If the response is negative, or not what you hoped, that's fine. All that means is that you are at a dead end (at least as far as the enrollment process goes with this person). It's far better that you know early on. What you don't want is to continue to expect enrollment when it clearly doesn't make sense for him.

By contrast, when you have your sales hat on, and you *will* need to put your sales hat on, you want to get the potential customer to buy as well as enroll. The best salespeople are honest, but it is a functional kind of honesty. They are truthful about what their product or service does, but they accentuate the positive, especially the product's (or service's) financial advantage and how it fits the customer's needs. If they mention shortcomings, they both minimize them and put them in the best possible light.

However, getting people to enroll requires a deep honesty about aspirations and values. It's generally not about functionality or money. People enroll with *you*, perhaps even more than with your vision. That's why you tell the complete truth. And they will either join you or not. That is just the way it goes. There's nothing you can do to *get* someone to enroll. When you try, you'll invariably become manipulative and start selling your vision. The person you are trying to sell will see right through it. People can immediately sniff out when you are trying to get them to do something, even if it is in their best interest. There is no reason to go down this road when what you are looking for is genuine commitment to your cause. People either want to enroll or they don't.

Let's suppose the person you are talking to gets excited. Well, of course, this is a good thing, but often only part of the equation. Yes, she may be excited for you. She may be happy that you have found something that feels right for *you*. But it does not mean that she is willing to join you. She will enroll only when what you have talked about connects to a desire within *her*. And the deeper the connection between what you are talking about and what is important to her, the more likely she is to put her shoulder to your wheel alongside you. And, fortunately, that happens fairly frequently. When it does, you end up discussing what is important to both of you. At that point, your vision clarifies and actually changes, even if only a bit, to become *our* vision. (For an example of how one organization handles the issue of enrollment, see the discussion of Willow Creek Community Church in the box, "Enrolling Believers.")

## Enrolling Believers

Perhaps no one deals with the issue of enrollment better than the Willow Creek Community Church, a nondenominational, evangelical megachurch in Illinois. More than twenty-three thousand people attend one of its three services every weekend.

How has the church grown so big? The church believes that conversion can only come if you enroll someone in your mission. The first step in that enrollment is to form a relationship of authenticity with the person you are trying to get to come along.

You are probably not going to forge an authentic relationship by sending someone a video or having her come to your Web site or read your book. So from the beginning, the church rejected the notion that you could somehow get someone to enroll through electronic or written means. People join the church through having an authentic relationship with someone who cares—that is, someone who is truly enrolled himself—in this case, someone who is already a member of the Willow Creek Church.

The first step in the relationship usually has nothing to do with the church itself. (Proselytizing is selling, and the church is not trying to gain buyers; it wants people to join its mission.) You, a member of the church, might become friendly with someone. If you got around to talking about religion, as friends sometimes do, you would talk about what you believe, and if your new friend seemed interested, you'd invite him to a Willow Creek service where he would be entertained, at the very least. Services, held in what is best described as a theater, are about an hour long; there is music, and the sermon is practical and doesn't involve guilt.

Your friend might attend a service or two. If he did, you'd give him time and space to determine for himself if he liked the church. If he concluded, "this is not for me," you would stop the enrollment process. (It's no different from an entrepreneur who is turned down by someone he is trying to enroll.) Your new friend would remain your friend, and you would look for other people who might want to join the church.

If your friend did express an interest in joining the church, you would invite him to take the next step in the enrollment process, which is to attend midweek worship, where biblical teaching occurs and the sacrament is served. And so it would go, if he continued to be interested.

At no point would there be sales pressure. People decide to enroll or they don't.

Although Willow Creek is now a huge church, the process works exactly the same way at a small church—or anywhere else for that matter. But since we began the example talking about churches, let's end it the same way.

Meet our friend Jessie Stone, who started out teaching Sunday School, gave the occasional guest sermon, and finally left, compelled to become ordained. But while he served as pastor at a number of churches in his native Oklahoma, he never truly felt at home. You could say he was not fully enrolled.

The thing Stone always liked best about church was songs. He loves "the standards." He loves the "new stuff. Heck, I even wrote some of my own." Stone fantasized about an all-singing service.

One day, he decided to do it. He invited some fellow parishioners ("hey, would you be interested in a church service that is 95 percent singing?") to attend on a Thursday night.

"Sounds good to us," a handful of people said. "Count us in."

They sang together for more than an hour. They repeated the idea the following week, and a few more people came. For the first time, Stone was fulfilled, and the people who came week after week found something that resonated with them.

It's been about a year now. Stone has started his own small church (in an empty store in town owned by one of the parishioners). About thirty people come each week, and another two thousand tune in via the Internet. There is thirty-five minutes of singing. Stone sermonizes for ten minutes, and everyone sings for another half hour, or more. Afterward, people hang around to enjoy each other's company and talk about the sermon.

## There Are Many Roles in Enrollment

Obviously, there are many different ways for people to become involved when they enroll with you. Sure, they may join your venture whole hog and make it the most important thing in their life. Conversely, they may contribute every once in a while, or fall somewhere in between.

Looking for an analogy? Think of election campaigns. Some people just stick a sign for the candidate on their front lawn. Others stuff envelopes, while the more committed might go door to door, or take time off and volunteer at the local campaign headquarters.

You need and should welcome each and every person because as she becomes enrolled, she will help spread the word about what you are trying to do.

## Step 3. Offer action

You will notice that an integral part of the enrollment process is to immediately offer the person who wants to join you some real work to do, no matter how small. There aren't open-ended commitments, such as "I will get back to you." That is the equivalent of thinking, not doing. As we said, there are many roles in enrollment, and you can propose a big part or a small one—depending on people's needs and yours. But an immediate offer is to your advantage and theirs so that you can take action together. When that action occurs, you know the enrollment has really taken place.

## The difference between selling and enrollment (and by the way, you need both)

If you are selling, you are trying to persuade, convince, influence, sway—whatever word you want to use—someone to do something you want them to do. You want someone to buy what you have.

---

### Spreading the Word

This is implicit in everything we have talked about so far, but we think it is worth flagging.

If you make a "sale," news of what you are trying to accomplish may or may not spread beyond the person you sold to. That person may tell one other person or maybe a couple of others, if she is extremely pleased, but she may not.

If someone enrolls, the propagation of your message is virtually assured. It's like the circles that form when you throw a pebble into a lake. The person who enrolls tells as many people as he can. Some of those people enroll and they tell as many people as they can and so it goes.

---

Honest selling is a noble profession. Great salespeople can make your life easier when you are looking to buy. But while a great salesperson wants you to be happy, her ultimate focus is on getting you to do what she wants: buying. Her goal is to make the sale, a transaction of real things (her goods or services for your money).

In contrast, when someone enrolls, it is because you have inspired him to act in favor of what *he* wants to do. It is an exchange of intangibles. You can't buy anybody's commitment. You can buy his product—and he can buy yours (and again, that is perfectly legitimate)—but you can't buy commitment. He becomes part of your efforts because he is excited by your dream and wants to join you. The essence of enrollment is that your efforts become his efforts as well. (The differences between sales and enrollment are shown in table 6-1.)

That's the key distinction between enrollment and selling. Ultimately, you want both. Sales without enrollment yield a customer.

TABLE 6-1

### Differences between selling and enrollment

|  | Selling | Enrollment |
|---|---|---|
| Essence | Commercial transaction, i.e., an exchange of real things | Emotional or spiritual transaction most similar to an exchange of gifts. |
| Process | Selling or persuading | Inspiring or sharing |
| Tools | Cost-benefit analysis | Conversations |
| Who is the other person | They are either a customer or they are not | Everyone |
| The other's desire to support you | Can be minimal or nonexistent | Essential |
| Propagation, i.e., what happens when the initial encounter is complete? | Maybe nothing. It can be a one-off transaction. | Broad. The person who is enrolled spreads the message. |

That is good, but perhaps it is a missed opportunity (the customer might have spread the word about you). Enrollment without a sale creates ambassadors. That's good, too. But could you have "taken their order" as well? When you have enrollment with sales, you have a home run.

Here's an example, involving an unlikely source: QVC, the on-line shopping channel, where the on-air "talent" tries to sell you merchandise.

The hosts are not scripted, because the network wants the sales pitches to be as friendly and authentic as possible. In preparation, the network puts presenters in a room where they get to play with the merchandise; they are given the demographics of who the product is likely to appeal to and then they're asked to figure out a way to sell it. One of the most effective salespeople, bar none, was a former high school Spanish teacher, Kathy. How she sold computers will make our point.

QVC had failed miserably when it first tried to sell computers, back when personal computers were just being introduced. Like everyone else, it had tried to sell computers on the basis of capabilities—bits and bytes, storage, and the like. Unless someone truly understood how the machines worked—and let's face it, most of us didn't, and still don't—he was not going to plunk down $2,100 for a machine based on its specs.

Kathy took a different approach. At the beginning of her hour, she walked onto the set with a sealed box. Inside, she said, was exactly the same computer you would receive if you ordered. She more or less said, I am your friend, Kathy and over the next half hour I am going to explain to you how I realized this computer is one of the most important things you can have in your life.

As she began talking, a man walked onstage and began to take the computer out of the box. She introduced him and said, Steve is going to put the computer together while we talk. You will see the hardest thing about getting the machine up and running is getting it out of all the packaging.

Then Kathy began discussing the product. She started by saying she knew nothing about computers. But what she did know was that there was an entirely new world you could connect to if you had one. (As an aside, Kathy as you will see is also a great master at establishing acceptable loss and helping people act quickly.)

She had this thing beautifully timed. She talked about what computers could do, stopping every once in a while to talk to Steve to underscore how simple the set up was. At the twenty-seven-minute mark, there was a computer booted up and fully functioning, and the camera zoomed in so you could watch her surfing the QVC Web site.

Her viewers said, "Wow, Kathy just did this. I can do this." In the next half hour, Kathy basically reviewed what she had done, and by the time the hour was up, QVC had sold millions of dollars worth of computers with virtually no returns. That was millions in sales simply by creating a fundamental relationship of authenticity coupled with selling. She was authentic. She talked about how she was a novice. And she showed every step in the process.

## *Just Start:*
## An Exercise for Enrolling People

Rewrite your desire as if it were fully accomplished and successful. What would it look like and feel like?

For example, say your desire is to throw a great party. In this case, your description might be: It's the end of the party. Guests are exhilarated and exhausted from laughing. People have grown closer. Some are actively planning a repeat event.

Tell a friend or someone else what you want to do, but spend most of your time describing what it will be like when your desire is fulfilled. Then ask, "Do you have any ideas to help? To make it better? People you might know who can help or contribute?"

## Takeaways

1. **Enrollment is getting people to buy in** and be excited along with you. It's a voluntary, personal commitment on their part.

2. **Selling** is getting someone else to do something that you would like him or her to do.

3. **You want both.** Sales without enrollment creates a customer, and that's fine. Enrollment without a sale creates people who talk positively about what you are trying to do. That's good, too. But when you have both, à la Kathy at QVC, truly remarkable things happen.

*Part Three*

# How This Works in the Real World

# 7

# View the Future Along a Continuum: When to Use Prediction and When to Use Creaction

By looking at the future in terms of the known and the unknown, you can determine whether to use Prediction or Creaction.

"HOW DO I KNOW WHEN TO USE CREACTION instead of Prediction reasoning?" If we had a nickel for every time someone asked us that question, we would have a very pleasant second income. The query goes to the very heart of what this book is about.

We'll start our answer by taking two scenarios as end points on a "continuum of knowability." (See figure 7-1.) Scientific advancement is made by moving things from the unknown ("the gods did it") to the known ("a bacterial infection did it"). So, those are our end points—the known and the unknown.

At the known end of this continuum are *completely predictable* things, such as things governed by physical laws. A small stone lying on the ground is just going to stay there unless some force (your foot)

**FIGURE 7-1**

is applied to it (and you kick it down the road). Or, in the case of levers, if you put a thirty-pound two-year-old on one side of a teeter-totter and a one-hundred-eighty-pound dad on the other side, the child will go up, not the dad. The outcome is certain.

Prediction is the logical choice in these cases, and doing and deciding on anything else is silly. (That darn stone is not going to move itself.) To quote one of our favorite philosophers, Damon Runyon, who wrote the stories that are the basis of the musical *Guys and Dolls*: "The race does not always go to the swift, nor the battle to the strong, but that is the way to bet."

At the other end—the unknown—is *completely unpredictable*. Nothing in the past or present will help you. Let's ask whether next Tuesday at 9:30 a.m., you will be struck by a brilliant idea that will transform your business. In trying to figure out if this is going to happen, Prediction isn't of much use, and using it is simply not logical. It could happen. But no one knows if it will.

In conditions of "maximum uncertainty," your best strategy is to take intelligent action and do what you can with what you have, which describes Creaction perfectly. It is actually the only logical choice, even though the outcomes of the actions you take might be completely unpredictable.

FIGURE 7-2

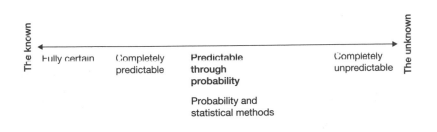

With the extremes established, let's return to certainty. There are stops along this continuum to certainty. Just after the point at which we are always certain of the outcome, there is *predictable through probability* (see figure 7-2). You know that you are never going to be able to roll a seven with a six-sided die, since the number is not there. (And if you roll it many times and it doesn't land almost equally on all six sides, you've learned something important about that die—it's likely to be loaded!)

Moreover, faced with a probabilistic situation, there are things you can do to nudge your predictions even further to the left on the graph, moving them closer to "fully certain." Maybe you can pay (a tiny) amount to gain additional data to determine whether the idea you are contemplating is something that is worthwhile. And if the additional data doesn't move you further along to the left, in the graphic above, you've learned something important as well. Knowing that you are not moving toward a more predictable situation can be as important as confirming that you are effectively in one. You will certainly not gain that knowledge through thinking alone.

For example, you are convinced that there is a market for a simple app that could tell people, literally at the push of a button, whether the restaurant entrée they are contemplating is healthy or unhealthy. Simple market testing would tell you that it is possible to create such an app, but very few people would download it because they have a pretty good idea of what is good or bad for them (and that they tend to err on the side of "I am going to be bad just this once," when they go out to eat).

You can employ other advanced predictive methods in other settings. For example, weather forecasting employs both chaos theory and computer modeling. Yet, even these are not perfect tools—as anyone who has been caught in an unexpected Midwest blizzard can tell you—but we do have history that enables us to make some predictions. (Yes, it could snow in Chicago in April, because it has in the past. But there is no record of it snowing in July.)

The same thing happens elsewhere. Insurance: we have tons of data telling us that specific areas have been flooded a number of times in the past. Actuarial: people die in certain patterns. If you need to answer questions like this, and you can do the analysis, use Prediction (see figure 7-3).

If you are not in one of these situations, it may make sense to act, provided the cost of getting started is low enough. (Or, you could learn how to do the analysis or pay someone who can, although this can be expensive in terms of time as well as money.)

Your strategy in probabilistic scenarios ("the vast majority of people in New England love the Red Sox. I wonder if hand-knit Red Sox tea cozies would sell?") is simply to calculate the odds; don't pay any more than the expected return over a number of tries or what the outcome is worth to you; and make sure you have enough money to stay in the game until the odds work in your favor.

**FIGURE 7-3**

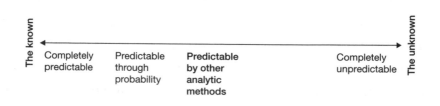

More specifically, the process would work like this:

Step 1. What are the chances this idea will work? (The answer informs step 2.)

Step 2. If you think, realistically, that this idea is a long shot—you have no idea whether your hand-knit Boston Red Sox tea cozies will be a hit—you don't want to invest very much. But since you've seen from experience that Red Sox fans buy *anything*, you're willing to increase what you'd pay to play a bit.

Step 3. But you don't want to increase it too far. To make sure the statistics work in your favor, you want to be able to stay in the game—which in this case means creating many iterations on your idea. (Maybe hand-knit beer-can insulators?) Why? On average, the more you play, the more you are likely to win in the long term, but you need to survive long enough in case the numbers don't break your way by the time they are mathematically supposed to. It's like gambling at the casinos, except in this situation, you want to be the casino.

## Moving on

One step further along the continuum is a place that is possibly predictable, but you have to *act* in order to find out. At this point, action becomes required to augment Prediction.

Here's an example. Assume that we give you an opaque jar containing an unknown number of dice with various numbers on the faces and ask you to bet on the sum of all of the faces when the dice in the jar are dumped out. Predictive math isn't going to help you very much. Yes, you know it has to be a positive number and it can't be incalculably huge unless the dice are immeasurably small and are twenty-sided. But that is about as far as Prediction can take you.

The only sensible way to find the answer is to act, provided the cost is low enough. In this case, it is. The first action, dumping the dice out of the jar, gives you a lot of knowledge you may not have had. For example, you can now estimate the total number of dice. (Of course, the appearance of new information may not be as stark in other situations.) Even if we don't let you count the number and the kinds of dice, the more you act—you dump the jar ten more times—the more you learn. A pattern can emerge and you are able to better predict future outcomes. ("Let's see, I dumped the jar repeatedly and most of the dice had six sides. And I guess that there are about 150 in the jar. That means the highest roll could not be more than about 900 and the lowest can't be below about 150. Just to hedge my bets on the count, I'll say there are 200 dice. So, the final number has to be between 200 and 1,200. The odds are against getting all ones or all sixes, and the first few dumps showed that; it produced pretty random results, and there are many more combinations of dice that yield 600 to 700 than there are those that yield 200, or 1,200. So I'd be far better off betting on 650 than 200, so that is what I am going to bet.")

Notice that in this scenario, your strategy must include action of some sort, at the very least to produce evidence that can lead to learning and better predicting.


## Moving toward the unknown

Further along the continuum are patterns that can't be derived analytically or predicted in advance, and yet you are still pretty good at figuring them out, even if you are not sure why.

It turns out that the human mind can often discern these patterns, but only through experience. These are situations where you are processing data in some way, even though you might not be able to articulate it. You are making decisions based on intuition, instinct, and experience. In this

FIGURE 7-4

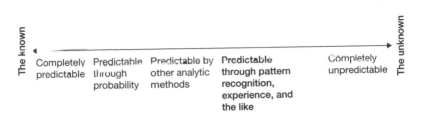

The known

Completely    Predictable   Predictable by   Predictable        Completely
predictable   through       other analytic   through pattern    unpredictable
              probability   methods          recognition,
                                             experience, and
                                             the like

The unknown

situation, there is no amount of schooling or study that will help you. Quite the contrary. Often, the more you study, the worse your performance gets. Overthinking in a situation like this (sports, riding a bicycle, improvising music) undermines performance. But *doing* it over and over again can lead you to a better performance. There is some sort of underlying rule, principle, or pattern. You may not be able to articulate it (you tell people who are amazed you got the right answer that you were acting on gut instinct), but you have come up with a way to discover it, even if it you are not able to write down your "recipe." (See figure 7-4.)

Examples abound. A famous tennis coach developed the ability to tell whether a second serve was going to be in or out the moment *before* the ball was struck by the racquet. He can't tell you how, nor can the people who have studied him with videos. Yet his ability is verifiable; he's able to do it in repeated tests with uncanny accuracy. Even the most advanced mathematics will not reliably predict which way a thrown Wiffle ball will break over the plate, yet a six-year-old can reliably hit it with a bat.

## Our advice?

So when should you use Prediction and when should you use Creaction?

- **In situations that are predictable, predict.** Acting when you can make a successful prediction instead is a waste of resources. It's unwise unless the cost of action is quite low.

- **The more unpredictable, the less logical it is to use Prediction and the more logical it is to use Creaction**, that is, smart action. Intelligent action basically means, how do I reduce the cost of the action (experiment) I want to take to find out what I need to know?

- **The less predictable a situation is, the less you should be willing to pay to play** (see chapter 4) for outcomes of equal value. To illustrate: you would probably bet up to $.49 on a coin flip when you would get a dollar back if you got it right. And you'd want to be sure you had a few bucks in your wallet to cover the possibility that it may take a few flips for the odds to begin to net out in your favor. You'd only pay about $.16 on the roll of the six-sided die, if the bet involved picking which of the six numbers would come up, in return for $1. And you'd probably pay even less betting on the outcome of the rolling of all the dice in that opaque jar that we described earlier.

- **Desire mediates (offsets) what you are willing to pay to play.** The more you want something, or the more you are at least curious about it, the more you would be willing to pay to take a step toward it. This is pretty obvious. (See figure 7-5.)

**FIGURE 7-5**

**What you are willing to pay to play**

Completely predictable

With desire

Completely unpredictable

Without desire

- **You are using Prediction everywhere along this continuum, including when you are creacting.** It sounds strange, but it's true. Whenever you are creacting, you are predicting. Virtually every action implies a prediction of what you think will happen. Even in situations of maximum uncertainty, you are making predictions about what can't happen. In predictable situations, Prediction tries to establish what will be in the set of possible outcomes. In unpredictable settings, it tries to rule things out in the hope of estimating the attractiveness of that which remains. ("I don't necessarily know what the prize is going to be but I know it can't be this and that improves my odds.") (See figure 7-6.)

**FIGURE 7-6**

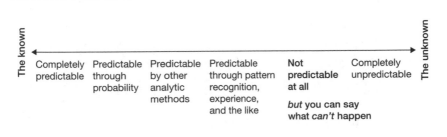

- **Even in extreme predictability, acting can make more sense than more thinking.** (See "The Case of the Unbroken Egg.") If you think back to chapter 1, you will understand why in the face of extreme predictability, acting can make more sense than thinking. In chapter 1, if we asked you to take an egg, hold it at arm's length, and drop it on your tile floor, you'd predict very confidently—based on prior experience—that it would break. We don't have to do the calculation. If we asked you to fill your bathtub with water, hold an egg out at arm's length, and drop it into the bathtub, would you predict that it is going to break? (You wouldn't, right?) What if you dropped the egg from two stories up into a swimming pool? Most of us don't instantly know if the egg will break. If an egg were really expensive, we could begin to research the question on the Internet. And there are certainly people who could do the analysis—they'd determine the velocity of the egg when it hit the water and compare that to the impact necessary to break an eggshell, and so on.

## The Case of the Unbroken Egg

A friend of ours could perform, or gain access to, all the calculations we just talked about, but when he was on vacation in the Caribbean, he simply got curious. The next time he went to the beach, he took an egg out of his refrigerator and dropped it into the ocean from arm's length. It didn't break. So our friend (and we) are pretty certain that he could drop it in a bathtub without breaking it. (Of course, with more drops with different kinds of eggs, we would become more certain.)

Then he threw it as high in the air as he possibly could and he learned two things. First, it is very hard to throw an egg straight up, and second, it still doesn't break when it hits the ocean water, or at least this one didn't.

Again, our friend could have done the research, but if he had no engineering skill or Internet skill, it would have taken a lot of his time to learn to figure it out. But he did figure it out—by acting. This situation has now become more predictable ("you know what, if you drop an egg into water from a height of 20 feet or less, it probably won't break"), and he learned it cheaply by simply dropping the egg.

Even in the case where things might be utterly predictable and analyzable, sometimes it is cheaper and faster just to act.

- **Action always leads to evidence and learning; thinking does not,** even in an extreme case where you try something that you think is utterly predictable given physical laws. If it turns out as predicted, you have confirmatory evidence ("Hey, my high school physics teacher was right!"), even if no new learning. But if something unexpected happens, the result is that you know something is seriously wrong or very unusual, and that's something no one else on the planet may know. In science, an experiment that turns out differently than expected is often welcomed and treasured because it leads to a new line of inquiry.

- **Prediction incurs costs that are often overlooked.** For example, it forestalls the benefits of early action. (Of course, more Prediction might forestall a preventable error. It's a trade-off that rests on judgment and acceptable loss.) Taking action lets you get evidence right now and increases your chances of getting started sooner. ("I can enter the market ahead of any competition. More importantly, whatever ultimate economic benefits there are to my action, they arrive faster and they last longer because I have several months or years of income at the front end that I would not have if I had spent the time predicting.")

- **As we have seen, some things are predictive or creactive by nature,** but most projects move from uncertain to more certain as they progress. So you use elements of both Prediction and Creaction all along the way, but the emphasis is different at different times.

- **It's all very personal.** Predictability is rarely absolute. What is unknown for you might well be known by someone else. The question is not so much whether something is predictable or not, it's whether it is predictable by you.

*When you add all this up, therefore, asking whether to use Prediction or Creaction is the wrong question.*

Creaction should always be considered as an alternative or at least a complement to Prediction.

Creaction should always be considered as an alternative or at least a complement to Prediction in part because Creaction may be more logical in a particular situation, even though that situation is predictable.

We are so habituated to Prediction that the disciplined questioning of using Creaction is a good idea. It leads us to a bias toward intelligent action to offset the habit of Prediction and better coordinate these two, very valuable kinds of thinking.

TABLE 7-1

## Contrasting Prediction and Creaction

| Prediction | Creaction |
|---|---|
| **View of the future** | |
| The future is a continuation of the past and can be reasonably predicted. Accuracy of prediction is paramount. | The future is contingent on human action. Unpredictability itself is seen as a resource. |
| **Desire** | |
| Desires are fulfilled by extrapolating from the past and optimally positioning yourself to exploit it. | Desires are fulfilled by doing the doable and continually transforming current realities into new and unforeseen possibilities. |
| Do what you "should" do based on what's "best," often as defined by others. | Do what you want and are able to do, which is not necessarily "best." |
| **Basis for commitment and action** | |
| **Goals and plans** determine what resources you acquire. "What means do I need to assemble to achieve these goals?" | **Means at hand.** "What effects can I create with the means I have?" |
| **Think and plan.** Act only once the logic is fully in place to achieve the end. Every step is based on the previous step in the plan. Thorough analysis precedes action. Time and/or other resources are invested in upfront information gathering. | **Start acting as soon as you can,** as soon as it's logical to take the next step. Each next step is based on the new reality that results from your action. |
| **Attitude toward investment and risk** | |
| **Expected return.** Calculate upside potential and pursue (risk-adjusted) best opportunity. Carefully avoid failure. | **Acceptable loss.** Calculate downside potential and invest no more than you want or can afford to lose. Keep failures small and have them happen early, and then learn from them. |
| **Dealing with the unexpected** | |
| **Bring plan back on track.** | **Redesign plan** and sometimes even your desires in order to profit from surprises. |
| **Attitude toward others** | |
| **Transaction.** Who you bring on board and the subsequent relationships with customers, suppliers, or others is governed by what is necessary to achieve the stated goals. | **Co-creators.** Build your market together with customers, suppliers, and even prospective competitors. The people who come on board help determine the goals and shape of the outcome. |
| **Summary logic** | |
| **To the extent we can predict the future, we can control it.** | **To the extent we can create the future, we do not need to predict it.** |

*Source:* Modified from an original source of Sarasvathy.

The question of whether to use Prediction or Creaction is inappropriately framed for another reason. The question itself implies that an answer to it will more predictably lead to success. But by definition, we are talking about situations where Prediction is illogical, so how can we be sure any answer about which mode of thinking to employ will be right? Said another way, if you find yourself in a realm that you have characterized as not having known or knowable rules, then a rule about what to do when you are there doesn't make much sense. As soon as you're really into unpredictable territory, you can't form very good predictive rules about what to do, which includes whether to use Prediction or Creaction.

Our metaphor for dealing with this is bilingualism. People who can speak two languages know certain things are better expressed in one language than another. For example, when a friend of yours is going on a long trip, you could say in English, "Good-bye and good luck." But others of us think, *Vaya con Dios*, which literally translates to "go with God," is a much better way of saying it.

Certain things are better expressed in one language than another. It's a great thing to be able to use the right word or the right language to fit the situation. Which to use, Prediction or Creaction, follows the same logic: figure out what the situation demands and use the right tool (reasoning, in this case) for the job.

## Using Prediction and Creaction together

You can imagine, or perhaps you know, the kind of person who always acts first and thinks later. He doesn't ever want to think anything through. His approach to everything? "Hey! What feels good in this moment?" And he acts. There is a range of situations where that's probably intelligent and another (larger) range of situations where it is probably pretty darn dumb.

The counterpart is the person who is so completely wedded to thinking things through that she will sit and think when the smart thing to do is just act. She doesn't act because she doesn't have that orientation in her repertoire.

Putting this together, you get a picture of a full range of situations in which we live—from places where you should be predicting (and those people who don't predict very well ought to learn how) to those situations where prediction is going to do you no good whatsoever. In those cases, you need to learn to act, and act "smartly," which means as quickly and with as little cost as possible. Discerning what to emphasize is the challenge, since we are trained and habituated to prefer thinking to acting.

When faced with any situation where you find yourself responding by thinking, it is good to notice where along the predictability spectrum you think you are and ask, "Is there any way for me to act in this situation?" If there is, the questions become: "Is there a way for me to act quickly and at acceptably low cost that will get me more or better information or put me further ahead than sitting and thinking about this anymore? What would constitute a relatively quick, smart, low-cost action in this situation?"

Here are three examples.

In the first, you are toying with an idea, but you don't really know what it is yet. The idea may eventually be something that predictive thinking can be applied to, but that's in the future. At this point, you aren't even sure how to frame it. In this case, and with apologies to Nike, just doing something helps form the idea. Draw it, talk it out, whatever. But act! Don't continue trying to intellectualize it.

In the second example, you may have an idea, and the idea may in fact eventually benefit from traditional testing. But, before getting to that point, you need to learn more. In this situation, even though prediction is valid, taking action gets you up the learning curve faster. Howard Schultz had an idea for starting European-style coffee houses. So he tested one that had servers in tuxedos and Italian opera playing in the background. Folks did not like the frills, but they loved the coffee.

In the third example, you have all the resources in the world to predict, but you have an idea that will allow you to get up the implementation curve much faster. The story of Malcolm Collins illustrates our point. He sold a software company that he and his partner Pete had started and decided to take some time off. After a while, he got tired of people asking him, "What are you going to do next?" He had been a home brewer for twenty years, so he started answering, "I'm going to start a microbrewery." He wasn't particularly serious, but it was a convenient way to answer people's questions.

After a while, Gary, a lifelong friend and marketing and strategy consultant, got tired of listening to Malcolm talk about this fictional brewery and implored him to "just do it. And, I'll do it with you!" Pete jumped on board, too, and so did another friend, Larry, who loves selling.

The guys played with a couple of concepts—they nixed the idea of adding a restaurant, given the high failure rate of places that serve food—and they really didn't see why they needed to make the beers themselves. What about selling English-style ale on draft? That's what they liked to drink, but the ales were hard to find in Seattle where they all lived.

They could have gone the traditional (Prediction) route and done market research, testing to see if there was a potential market. They had more than enough money and experience to go that way, had they wanted to. But they wanted to learn by doing. They called a bunch of bars and restaurants in the Seattle area to find out what the level of interest was. It seemed pretty strong, so they used the Internet to put together a list of ideal partners in England. The number-one criterion was to have won a major award.

The guys jumped on a plane for a week's "vacation" in England. Several pub crawls later, they selected the brand Freckled Johnson's and worked out a licensing deal. They came back to Seattle, contracted a local microbrewery to whip up a batch for them, and then wandered around to various bars in the area and got a few of them to stock it.

Their business was effectively up and running in a matter of weeks (albeit at a low level), and they had a local supply of the English ales they all loved. If they had gone the Prediction route, it could have taken a year or more before they could get a draft.

The key idea here is clear. There will be situations in which the future will be fairly knowable. But, often you will find yourself at a point in the process where learning is more important than predicting, and you can best get the learning by doing.

## *Just Start:*
## An Exercise for Deciding When to Use Prediction and When to Use Creaction

All of this theory is great, but how do you actually decide in real life?

Whenever you seek to form a new habit or change an old one, it takes a certain amount of self-awareness. Sometimes you catch yourself right at the beginning. You have an idea for something you want to create. Ask yourself how unknown the field you will be playing on is? How much latitude do you have to learn in this situation? The answers to these questions will give you good information on the applicability of Creaction to your situation.

Other times, you awake to find yourself totally immersed in Prediction-based implementation. Here (as in the first situation), try these questions:

- Instead of thinking some more, is there an action I can take right away?

- Can I make whatever action I just imagined cheap enough so that it lies within my acceptable loss?

The point here is that you may or may not actually take the action, depending on your ultimate judgment. But asking the question(s) interrupts and sheds light on your thinking habits.

Self-awareness develops over time. And over time, you are also trying to teach yourself that Prediction is not the only option in a given situation. Creaction is often an available option and, in certain cases, more valid.

Changing the way you approach problems can feel awkward, unfamiliar, and even threatening. Two suggestions: Fully imagine yourself taking the unfamiliar road. See how it feels. Then see if you can be comfortable with that discomfort, if it's there. And as always, talking this through with a friend is a really good idea.

## Takeaways

1. **It is rarely either/or.** While there are some things—like gravity on earth—that are absolutely certain, a great number of things are not. Similarly, you can find places where you simply can't predict what will happen, but you often can take small steps toward finding out.

2. **What follows from point one** is that in the majority of situations you face, you will want to use Prediction and Creaction together simultaneously.

3. **Force yourself.** Prediction reasoning is almost everyone's default position, given that it is the way we all have been taught since kindergarten. Make a conscious effort to use Creaction everywhere.

# 8

# Preparing for Uncertainty: How to Use Creaction at Work

Traditional organizations are based on the assumption that the future is going to be very much like the past. Yet, a quick glance at the headlines shows that the world is seemingly growing more unpredictable each day. How can you introduce Creaction into the last place on earth set up to embrace it—the contemporary organization? It isn't easy, but it can be done.

I**T IS ONLY NATURAL** to mentally picture *large* organizations, such as *Fortune* 500 companies, when you read the word *organization*. And certainly, everything we are about to discuss is applicable to them. But everything we are going to discuss here also holds true for family businesses, nonprofits, and any other group of any size. For example, think about the challenges they face:

- They are trying to grow and create new products or services in a marketplace that becomes more competitive by the day.

- Most would like their business model to work better.

- All want to do more with less and deal better with uncertainty.

Obviously, Creaction could be a useful tool for dealing with these challenges. How to do that in every case is far too ambitious for this book. (We promise it will be the subject of a subsequent effort.) So our primary focus here is on how you as an individual can use Creaction to implement initiatives within your organization.

And let us say this up front, whether you are trying to be Creactive yourself or help your subordinates, it is a daunting task. Everything about contemporary Western organizations is designed to generate predictable performance. That's especially true for public companies. The market grants a premium to firms with smooth earnings as opposed to volatile ones (even when the long-term average performance is the same). So the need for consistent, unsurprising results gets incorporated into every aspect of the enterprise—the formal (and informal) structures, systems and processes, habits, norms, decision-making criteria, and so on—with the ultimate aim of achieving better shareholder value. These places deal in expected returns, not acceptable loss.

And you have to vault more than financial hurdles. Organizations default to "staying on plan," as opposed to building on what they find in the marketplace. They deny (or at least disregard) the power of desire, and instead treat people as fungible resources whose individual wants are subordinated (if included at all) to what the organization needs, that is, what its strategy calls for.

You can see how all this plays out when you think of the sorts of questions you always face if you propose an idea that even contains a modest level of uncertainty inside a company (or a nonprofit). At the very least, you will hear things like:

- Will it fit with our strategy?

- Will it ultimately be big enough and profitable enough to meet our larger organizational goals?

- What about the opportunity cost? How can we afford to divert the resources of our people to something with such unknown potential?

- What about the risks to other products or programs? Could they be cannibalized?

- Will this somehow damage our brand or public image?

- How do we know it will work better than what we have? The existing way seems fine to me.

Answers to all these questions require Prediction.

## Obstacles all around

It's not just the formal questions and hurdles that conspire to keep Creaction from fitting comfortably within companies and other organizations; there are the informal ones as well. Think of the number

### The Erosion of Ultimate Potential

For every predictive "checkpoint" you pass, the potential positive impact of a project or proposal gets reduced.

Consider what happens as your project runs the gauntlet of predictability. You get rid of the uncertain future paths and reduce your proposal to the most likely, predictable result that can then be economically evaluated. You end up bringing forward *only* the most likely proposal (not necessarily the one with the biggest potential, because the latter can't be known, nor do we have the same level of confidence that it will come to pass).

But each time you scrub out one of these currently less certain (or even unknown) options from your proposal, you rule out a potentially unlimited upside. This decision-making process virtually assures that any initiative will bear less fruit than it might have.

of departmental approvals companies typically require before implementing anything new; the number of presentations, and the number of adjustments, tweaks, fixes, and upgrades before any action is taken.

---

There's a good reason Prediction is pervasive in modern organizations: it works when the future is knowable or at least partially so.

But when the future is uncertain, Creaction works best. And organizations—and everyone else—should always use the right tool for the job.

---

If this weren't enough, there are the informal habits, procedures, and structures. In many organizations, you have to brief anybody whose area will be affected by your idea. You have to prepare and deliver each of these briefings (taking time away from actually doing anything). Just about everyone you brief can kill the idea—either overtly or simply through inaction—even though most of the people you will be talking to don't have the authority to approve it. Worse, many of those people will be biased toward killing your idea since the consequences of whatever you are proposing are unknown (or would require resources to estimate). So the "safest" decision is to just say no (or nothing).

Whether you are trying to employ Creaction yourself or encourage someone else to use it, any one of these factors can and often will kill your efforts. Taken together, they are lethal to anything that you cannot confidently predict to be successful.

So that's your starting point. Prediction is pervasive in modern organizations because it is effective in predictable (or partially so) environments. Much of the world has been and will continue to be predictable to some degree. And yet:

- Just about all organizations, at least some of the time, require the proverbial out-of-the-box thinking.

- All of them must deal with great uncertainties (at least sometimes).

- Traditional efforts to instill entrepreneurialism and innovation within organizations have been spotty at best, so they are looking for different approaches.

All this adds up to the fact that your task is not hopeless when you try to change how your organization does business. So, where do you begin? Let's start with what *not* to do.

## The *wrong* direction

Historical approaches to introducing new ideas to or changing an organization have often followed a straightforward path:

1. Determine where you want to be—in our case, a company that uses Creaction when appropriate or at least on your project.

2. Determine how close the organization is to the goal (probable answer: "Not very").

3. Chart a course between where you want to be (a project or organization that uses Creaction) and where you are now (one that does not).

4. Install some sort of reward system, support, and training that would allow the change to happen.

5. Add metrics that will chart the progress toward the goal and identify when things are getting off course.

6.  Launch and then do remedial work as necessary until the objective is reached.

Sounds familiar, doesn't it? It should. It's perfect Prediction. This route might involve more use of Creaction, but it probably won't. And you probably won't like the journey very much. There are three reasons why.

First, experience and research has shown that trying to change things like culture or decision-making processes with this type of process is labored at best and often flat out fails. While the analogy is clichéd by now, it is also true: organizations, like the human body, tend to reject foreign bodies inserted into them. And, as we have seen, Creaction is about as foreign as you can get when it comes to the way established companies do their business.

Second, the process we outlined could take months or maybe years.

Third, by going down this path, you run the risk of undermining the Prediction skills within your organization. That would be a huge mistake. Even though the universe grows seemingly more unpredictable by the minute, there are—and always will be—a huge number of things, maybe even the majority, which are predictable, and you don't want to weaken or eliminate a superior skill (Prediction) that the organization has, one that is effective under the right circumstances.

## The Why, When, and Where of Creaction in Organizations

Why use Creaction in organizations? Success with out-of–the-box innovation is spotty at best. This alternative has worked well for people who must deal with uncertainty every day: entrepreneurs. (There is nothing more uncertain than trying to create something that has never existed before.)

When to use Creaction? In situations when predictive methods just don't make a lot of sense.

Where to use Creaction? In product or service innovation, business model innovation, and perhaps across the entire organization.

Clearly, the historical approach is not appropriate when you want to introduce new ideas or change. If you want to use Creaction successfully, you are going to need to take a different approach.

Let's talk about the steps you might take.

## What can you do as a single employee?

So you want to show—teach may be a better way of putting it—your organization that Creaction is a viable tool. What do you do? First, realize that the learning has to occur on two fronts—on the individual (you) *and* organizational levels (your boss, peers, and subordinates).

You need to say, "Instead of butting my head against the wall trying to get the organization to accept this new way of thinking, my starting point needs to be how do I develop the ability to know when I should be leaning more heavily into Creaction?" You need to develop the ability to know when using Creaction is the right course of action. (Chapter 7 can help a great deal.)

In other words, as you face any new situation, ask yourself: "Is this a challenge I have seen before, and/or one where I am likely to know what is going to happen? If it is, I should probably employ the Prediction skills I have been trained to use for years. There is absolutely no reason to go down the Creaction path."

But if that is not the case—"in this situation, the future is basically unknowable"—then it makes sense to start thinking about employing Creaction.

When you do, you act exactly as you would if you were on your own as an entrepreneur. You would say, "Okay, so this really is an exercise in knowing who I am, who I know, what I know, getting things done through my personal networks, and doing everything in a way that absolutely minimizes the cost."

This is an argument for being clever and looking for innovative ways to work within the bounds of your own and your organization's acceptable loss. That way, if someone discovers and objects to what you are doing and the seeming lack of logic behind it, you can point out that the risk to the organization is minimal, while the upside could be huge.

Unless you are CEO, or a member of the C-suite at the very least, you generally can't convince your organization to create a new structure, but you can persuade it to perhaps attack a given problem from an unusual angle. ("Hey, boss, can we think about this one a different way?") You can do that, especially if you follow up with a way to save the organization money or operate more efficiently. (More on this later.)

You can complain, "I don't have any leverage; I can't change the cubicles, I can't rewrite the reward system and everything else." And the answer is, "No you can't; don't even try." But simply through your own thinking and getting other people to think differently, you can have enormous impact without changing any of that stuff.

The simple fact is "smart is smart," and we're talking about you offering an additional way of viewing problems. You'll never get in real trouble for doing that, especially if you do it gently by saying, "Can we think about this differently?"

So that is the first kind of learning that has to take place to introduce Creaction into the organization, the learning you have to do.

The second kind is organizational learning. You ask, "How do I make the organization (at least the part of it that is around me and what I want to do) hospitable to Creaction? What do I need to do to convince people that an additional way of thinking could be helpful, and that Creaction is a tool we should employ under the right circumstances?"

There is no recipe for this. We're dealing with something that is essentially a creative act, and consequently each organization has to handle it in its own unique way. If the company looks to adopt another company's version, it's because it's leaning right back into predictive thinking, that is, "If I imitate them somehow, it will be good for me."

Imitation will probably not be very successful, for at least two reasons. First, as of this writing, no large organization has formally adopted Creaction, so the places where it is being used are ad hoc and functioning within the unique confines of that organization.

Second, no two organizations are exactly the same, so what works well in one will not necessarily work in another. The upshot? You can learn from what others have done, but you can't adopt their methods completely. You need to put your own spin on it. Wholesale copying isn't going to work. One size does not fit all. Your organization is different from any other, as are you.

---

How should an organization act in the face of uncertainty?
By blending Creaction and Prediction.

---

What follows—with the most sincere apologies to Stephen R. Covey, is our current list of the seven habits of successful organizational creactionists. Whether you are a budding creactionist or a manager of one, you should remember this list of tactics as you try to employ Creaction in your organization:

1. **Link what you want to do to your firm's a business imperatives.** This is just about always fatal if it is overlooked— and it generally is. That's a shame since it is so easily addressed. Yes, of course, the idea of the rocket backpack that will allow us to fly to work is exciting, but if you work for a company that makes ball bearings, it is hard to see the fit. You want to begin the conversation by being able to say something

like this, "You know, the organization has the business goals of A, B, and C. (You can talk about organizational goals—such as improving teamwork—as well, but odds are you will find a more receptive audience if you start with business goals.) I've got an idea that I think will fit perfectly."

2. **Produce obvious, "local" business results.** Don't focus on organizational or cultural change. Prove the efficacy of your idea in the vocabulary and currency of your organization. Sure, it would be nice if you could change your organization into the next Google overnight, a firm that is willing to go wherever the market takes it. But if your boss's goal is to have the highest performing region in the company, that (à la point number 1) is the place to focus your attention.

3. **Make sure there is sufficient autonomy.** The unit(s) or individuals that use Creaction need to have enough freedom to be different and protected from the "restorative forces" the organization will impose (even in spite of itself). What this means for you and your project is this. Don't worry about getting everyone committed. You don't need to. There are four postures people can adopt: keep it from happening, let it happen, help it happen, and make it happen. Obviously, you don't want anyone in the "keep it from happening mode," if you can avoid it. But most people simply have to "let it happen." You (and possibly a few others) have to "make it happen." Your boss and maybe a few others have to "help it happen" and create a buffer around you. So, rather than asking, "How do I get everybody committed to my idea?" keep asking yourself, "What is the *least* amount of commitment I need to move forward?" (See "What Can You as a Manager Do to Foster Creaction?") You probably don't need a lot of sign-off to get underway.

4.  **Have volunteers only, please.** An important and overlooked
    point is that only people with desire should play in the un-
    known. It's not a good idea to compel people to work on a
    Creaction initiative. If you do, at the first sign of pushback,
    they are likely to start looking for excuses to go back to doing
    "their real jobs" (in the way they have always done them).
    Changing anything is hard enough without working with
    people who aren't committed. (See our discussion about en-
    rollment in chapter 6.)

5.  **Don't make big "kickoff" announcements.** Initially focus
    your attention only on the people who need it, that is, the
    people who are going to help you implement your idea.

    They need to understand the principles of Creaction. Their
    boss and their boss's boss? Not so much. In other words, there
    is no forced-march training of groups, large or small, and
    certainly no organizationwide approach to teaching Creaction
    at this point.

6.  **Manage expectations.** In early phases, keep it low-key. Be
    relatively quiet and offer only enough public announcements
    to provide sufficient autonomy of the experimental units.
    Don't mislead people into thinking that things will change
    quickly or that their lives will be different (except for the
    people actually involved in the Creaction project). At all
    times, your mantra should be "underpromise and overdeliver."

7.  **Build on successes and manage pace and momentum.**
    Learn what works and what doesn't. Make sure you've got a
    little bonfire going before you spread the coals. Pick up a cou-
    ple of small wins before trying to go any further. The advan-
    tage of Creaction is that it does not require replacing any of
    the existing structures that work for predictable situations.

These must be left in place while selectively permitting the seeding of Creaction where it is warranted. As we have seen throughout, Creaction doesn't replace Prediction; it's an additional tool. You don't radically change the existing systems, because the organization will just resist your efforts. Initially, you simply add to what is already there.

This example, which strikes close to home for us, shows exactly how the seven steps work. Year in and year out, Babson College is recognized worldwide as one of the leading academic institutions in the teaching and studying of entrepreneurship. The college is also continually rated one of the best business schools in the United States and ranked as one of the world's leading executive education providers.

The problem was that for many students who wanted to attend, either as undergraduate or graduate students, Babson had only one campus, located in suburban Boston. If you wanted to learn at Babson, you needed to head to Wellesley, Massachusetts, which was not necessarily convenient, especially if you had a full-time job elsewhere in the country.

The obvious solution? Open another campus.

The obvious concern? If Babson set up shop on the West Coast—San Francisco seemed to make sense given there are literally thousands of innovative start-ups in and around the city (Silicon Valley is within easy driving distance)—would people enroll?

Faced with that question, people who employ Prediction would say: "Let's spend $100,000 on market research to find out if there is a market for Babson on the West Coast. If there is, we can then put together a marketing program, buy some advertising, set up an admissions office, and launch our satellite campus, something that will cost us another $100,000."

But people who employ Creaction would take a different tack. Using the logic of "let's take a small step immediately and see what happens," they would say, "Let's just start advertising and say we are accepting applications for the spring semester. It will cost the same $100,000 as a marketing study. If people don't come, then we know there is no market, and all we have lost is the $100,000 we would have spent on market research anyway. But if qualified students *do* apply and enroll, then we know there is a market. We will have saved $100,000 (the money we would have spent on market research). And we will be underway six months earlier."

That's exactly what the college did. Imagine a prestigious business school not doing traditional market research and instead offering its "Fast Track MBA" (an accelerated, part-time, twenty-four-month program designed for experienced professionals who want to advance their careers while simultaneously earning their degree), in early 2010. Enrollment exceeded expectations, and Babson now has a West Coast presence.

## What Can You as a Manager Do to Foster Creaction?

### Support your pilot teams

- Permit, encourage, coach, and protect your teams by creating and sustaining sufficient autonomy for them.

- Make sure they prove their ideas with actual results (that support the business imperative). Success will eliminate a lot of obstacles.

### Breed Creaction in the entire organization

- Permit, encourage, coach, and protect your early adopters.

- Propagate outward, first to opinion leaders.

- Manage acceptable loss. (See also the section, "How to introduce Creaction organizationwide.")

**Play your proper role as senior management**

- Permit and encourage Creaction to happen.

- Manage acceptable loss.

- Make sure you have people on Creaction projects who really want to be there to create positive energy and get you to your goal faster.

## Could you introduce Creaction another way?

People sometimes ask us about a possible alternative: "Wouldn't one path to introducing Creaction within organizations be to keep it self-contained? In other words, you would sequester your efforts to deal with or capitalize on the unknowable. You could do that by creating a wholly separate organization with different rules, processes, design, and so on."

Lots of organizations have tried the self-contained approach, but without universal success. Yet, year after year, the consultants' preferred recipe is to set up a little unit on the side and completely protect it from the parent. Even when it works, it has problems that are well known to any who have tried it, such as:

- How do you reintegrate the ideas, products, or services the unit develops into the parent company?

- Who is going to run this unit? (Obviously someone steeped in Prediction won't be a good fit, and even the most creative corporate citizens are unconsciously wedded to prediction-based reasoning.)

- How will the performance of the entity be evaluated? (Will it be held to predictable rates of return or unrealistically high hurdle rates, because the approach is seen as risky? Neither is helpful.)

Closely related to the sequestered concept is the idea of limiting the employment of Creaction to certain specific activities, such as pilot projects. While sometimes successful, they suffer from the same sort of difficulties of reintegration and leadership.

Neither approach is a real, permanent solution, because the parent company itself needs to operate, at least some of the time, in the face of unknowability. You may be able to relegate certain aspects of the business landscape to a separate unit, but not all of it. Reality is not that convenient.

Given this, you are left with the inescapable problem: how does the parent operate in the face of unknowability? Creaction, which is best suited to situations of uncertainty, is the solution. This is obvious if you play out what happens when you try to apply the Prediction tools when you are faced with uncertainty. Not only are the tools ineffective, but they carry a higher cost in two different ways. The first is in time and resources. Applying the wrong tool—Prediction—to a situation where it will not work simply wastes both. The second is that applying Prediction's standards of success to Creaction just doesn't make sense.

Here's an example of the disconnect that can result from using a traditional return on investment requirement. A manager using Prediction says, "MegaGalatic's policy is that new products must produce a standard, acceptable return on investment and generate at least $25 million in additional revenue. The project under consideration (using Creaction) is pretty uncertain and we're not thinking about it in our normal, well-understood, and proven way, so we'd better hedge our bets and double the return we normally expect to adjust for this risk. And we'd better project at least $50 million in sales." Then she says, "Hmmm, now that I think about it, I am not sure that even that's enough. Let's double the safety margins."

Eventually, you get to the point where the hurdle rate is so high that the idea—no matter how promising—is never going to be approved. What's happened? A thinking process that is logical, rational, and a

## R-E-S-P-E-C-T the Boss (and Prepare to Vault These Three Hurdles)

Very early in the process of trying to introduce Creaction into the company you work for, you are going to run headlong into your boss. You have two choices. You can try to bulldoze your way through her. Or treat her as a respected colleague. You know which path is the right one to take.

Sketch out the long-term benefits of what you are proposing and then develop an acceptably low-cost next step. But, that is only step one. You also must put yourself in her Manolo Blahniks. You may have seen the light, but she could be skeptical. And there are three obstacles you are likely to face.

1. She knows something you don't that leads her to conclude a Creaction-based proposal won't work. You need to find out what that is and see if you agree.

2. Your proposal exceeds her acceptable loss—or her boss's. (You either figure out how to make that number smaller, or you are out of luck.)

3. She tells you what you are proposing won't be big enough. (This is, of course, totally a judgment call. While she gets paid for making it, you can argue—respectfully—that evidence is better than her intuition. And that evidence might be obtained with a few, low-cost steps well within acceptable loss.)

Respect (and having ready answers to these three objections) is what you need to get your boss on your side.

smart thing to do in a predictable universe gets unconsciously and habitually carried over and applied in an area where things are unpredictable. Not surprisingly, the results are far from ideal.

## Creaction Leads to a $5 Billion Company

Some huge companies owe their starts to Creaction. Clorox is one of them.

On May 3, 1913, five California entrepreneurs invested $100 apiece to set up America's first commercial-scale liquid bleach factory, which they located in Oakland, on the east side of San Francisco Bay. They called their product Clorox.

Surviving the early years was a struggle. Directors repeatedly extended personal loans to pay mounting corporate debts. In 1916, an early investor in the business, William C. R. Murray, was named general manager. Murray's wife, Annie, took on the responsibility of running their Oakland grocery store in his absence.

On Annie's request, Murray ordered plant chemists to develop a less concentrated household version of the industrial-strength Clorox bleach formula, and Annie gave free samples to her customers.

The household bleach solution, bottled in fifteen-ounce amber-glass "pints," quickly gained popularity as an effective and reliable domestic laundry aid, stain remover, deodorant, and disinfectant.

Impressed by the results of Annie's giveaways—she was receiving inquiries and requests for the product from as far away as the East Coast and Canada—the company adopted her tactic as a primary marketing tool. Retailers were instructed simply to hand out three of every four bottles free. They were fully reimbursed by the company. The people who tried the samples loved it and returned to pay full price.

By 1928, thanks to extensive national advertising and sales promotion campaigns stressing its purity, versatility, and dependability, the rubber-stoppered glass pint of Clorox bleach had become a commonplace sight in American laundry rooms, kitchens, and bathrooms.

The transformation of the industrial Clorox Company into a consumer packaged goods company was effectively complete.

We presume Annie asked for the household concentration because she wanted it. There was no reason at the time for Clorox to explore consumer goods. She began with the means at hand, her husband's ability to command the creation of a test product, essentially for free. The cost of the whole thing was well below anyone's acceptable loss. She used her partner's resources, The Clorox Company, for production. And Clorox then built each step it took (in the face of customer acceptance) into a national market.

Total sales of the company, which now also sells Pine-Sol cleaners, Fresh Step cat litter, Kingsford charcoal, and Glad bags and wraps and containers, among other consumer products, topped $5 billion in 2011.

## Why companies will embrace Creaction

Companies may be resistant to change. But they will (eventually) embrace anything that makes them a lot of money or helps it to advance. Creaction has the potential to do both. Here's what our Just Start course alumni and colleagues say when explaining the benefits of Creaction.

1.  Creaction will allow us not only to create new products, but also to create new business models, in contrast to just reacting to our competitors' new ones. (Wouldn't Blockbuster and the other stand-alone video rental stores have loved to have invented Netflix?)

2.  Creaction fosters taking initiative, since it favors quick, smart action and the concept of acceptable loss is built in. One of the current mantras we are hearing daily at our jobs is the desire for

employees to "take initiative." It is hard to do that in an organization that adheres strictly to Prediction. When we try to do something that doesn't work, we don't get fired, but people say, "You didn't think it through." That's perfect 20/20 hindsight, of course, but it only leads to more thought (to make sure that you do think it through), and less action the next time around.

---

If you want intelligent initiatives and/or potentially lucrative experiments, Creaction is for you.

---

3. Creaction provides a missing element—the foundation for leadership in the face of uncertainty. Our company is struggling with leadership and how to deal with uncertainty. Our tool kit is woefully incomplete and using Creaction helps fill it in.

Of course, this change can take longer than you like. If it does, simply channel some of your Creaction ideas elsewhere, while you are waiting. You don't give up hope; just go down another road simultaneously.

For example, Robin Vann Ricca was generally happy with what she was doing as head of organization development for the Home for Little Wanderers, a nonprofit child and family service agency in Boston. But despite strong effort, she felt that leadership development was one area that was not getting the organizational response she hoped for. She's passionate about the subject of leadership development in general and believed it could improve the organization in particular. She had hundreds of Creaction ideas she wanted to try, but somehow they never gained traction. So she was feeling a bit unfulfilled. But, instead of bemoaning the lack of change, she found an opportunity to use Creaction at her church.

Her pastor—young, vibrant, and full of ideas—noted the church's need for facilitation at an upcoming meeting. Ricca volunteered, and the pastor agreed. Their conversation (and her assignment) led to conversations about other church needs, including leadership development. Ricca ultimately developed a shared commitment for leadership development within the church. She can now use the tool kit developed in her church with other faith-based organizations she consults with and with the Home for Little Wanderers. Between her day job and her faith-based work, she is now considerably more fulfilled.

## How to introduce Creaction organizationwide

Since no one currently has any real experience introducing Creaction into large organizations, what we are suggesting will likely evolve over time. Based on our experience, following these steps would likely have the greatest chance of success.

Step 1. Instead of introducing the idea from the top down, one or a few early adopters need to employ the method on their own and see if it works for them on a real project.

Step 2. If it does, they need to use it again and share the results with the organization's thought leaders, who are not necessarily in formal leadership positions, but are the 5 percent to 10 percent of employees whose views receive a disproportionate amount of respect and attention. When thought leaders have or adopt an idea the entire organization accepts and endorses it. It becomes legitimate and goes viral.

Step 3. Formal leaders publicly support the efforts of these two groups—the early adopters and the thought leaders—or at the very least allow the approach to be used. It is not necessary for senior executives themselves to act creatively if they are genuinely supportive. Everyone knows these managers have a vested interest in keeping things the same. (They have thrived under the old system, which is why they are senior managers.) They are unlikely to change the behavior that has gotten them to the top. But they don't have to. All they have to do is help it happen or perhaps just let it happen. Don't wait for senior executives to take the lead.

These substantial steps could be enough to increase the likelihood Creaction will take hold and spread organizationwide over time.

Large organizations are skeptical about internal entrepreneurs—intrepreneurs—with good reason. Success with this concept has been spotty. We are not taking a position on intrepreneurship. We are arguing that large organizations need more entrepreneurial thinking, from every source possible.

## Just Start:
## An Exercise for Introducing Creaction into Organizations—
## The Crib Sheet

1. Learn to recognize when a particular setting has a high degree of essential unknowability, so the employment of Creaction is appropriate (and the employment of Prediction is not).

2. Develop a compelling next step with low acceptable loss (what will "get you further" in the shortest time, with the least resources) as an alternative to "more study."

3. Develop the capacity to enroll whatever sponsors, enablers, and approvers may be required. (Developing the ability to explain Creaction and why it is appropriate to those who are unfamiliar is especially important.)

4. Develop the personal desire and commitment to take that next step.

## Takeaways

1. **Think of airline advertising.** Airline commercials almost never show you the inside of the planes. They show where the planes can take you. In the same way, you don't want to advocate the virtues of Creaction. You want to show how the fruits of employing Creaction can benefit your company.

2. **Think bottom-up, one person at a time.** To be sure, change can start from the top down. The boss wants something done, so efforts are made to get it done. But for Creaction to take hold, it has to come from the ranks, rooted in individual initiative (tied to an organizational objective).

3. **Think Creaction.** Act with what you have at hand. Enroll and bring other people along.

4. **Take small steps.** Like mules, large organizations can take a long time to learn anything new. Don't expect overnight success in introducing a concept such as Creaction. Be prepared to take incremental steps.

5. **Don't waste your time if it's not something you care about.** Desire is important. Given how slow organizations are to change, be sure you are truly committed to the idea before getting underway.

# 9

# Using Creaction with Families and Friends

You can use Creaction outside of work to get things done. When you help family and friends to use Creaction, you will play one of two roles, as an actor or as a supporter.

T HE FOCUS until now has been on you, making sure you understand the logic that governs Creaction and how you can use it in beginning your new venture. But as we have shown throughout, starting a new business is not the only place you can apply Creaction. The same approach, principles, and logic that will help you start a new venture can also be used everywhere else. And everywhere else falls logically into two categories:

- Within organizations—the subject of the previous chapter.

- Outside of work, when you involve friends, family, and social and religious organizations, and within society in general.

Before we begin, some level setting about what's ahead. If you think about it, no matter where you find yourself in all the relationships we just listed outside of work, there is only one of two roles you could be playing. You are either:

1. An actor who is using the principles we have talked about and the others around you won't necessarily understand what you're doing or why you're doing it (and it would be handy for you if they did).

2. Part of the supporting cast. You are helping someone or a group of someones try to accomplish their goals.

We've come up with some general principles for each case, which will apply in all the situations. Let's take them one at a time.

## As an actor

In this situation, you are the person trying to get something done—helping your church, temple, or ashram (you think it would be a good idea if it worked with the women's shelter in town; getting your friends together to do something—anything—to improve your local schools; working with your family to figure out a way to honor a beloved relative).

To have these things happen requires you to develop your own capacity to use Creaction to the fullest, which means:

• Remembering the latent but perhaps forgotten capacity you have for Creaction; making a point to practice it on an ongoing basis in order to break the habit of overusing Prediction.

• Developing the ability to discern when a situation is, for your purposes, unknowable and therefore ripe for Creaction.

All of this ultimately occurs reflexively, rather like becoming effortlessly bilingual. People who are bilingual—kids are a great example—instinctually speak one language in one setting (English in school) and a second elsewhere (Spanish at home). They bounce back and forth, often within a sentence, with their friends who have the same language skills, using the Spanish word or phrase that is most evocative when it is appropriate and English when it is better. So somebody who is fluent in two languages unconsciously uses both to express his or her ideas. One is more dominant than the other, depending on the circumstances.

It can be exactly that way when you approach a problem in either your business or personal life: sometimes Prediction makes sense; other times Creaction does.

When you are the actor, you need to be able to explain to people, in terms they instantly understand, what you are doing and why. Three things can help you here:

- Always make the next step you want to take both compelling to the people you are speaking with and affordable. It's easy for people to understand why you're doing something when it sounds exciting and carries little cost or risk. (As a result, they are more likely to come along or support you.)

- Ensure that you really want to take that next step. You're not going to enroll anyone else if it's not something that is really meaningful to you.

- If you can, have a specific step in mind that people can take to contribute to your cause.

## As a supporter

In the situation where you're a supporting actor, your job is really to help other people take wise action. Or at the very least, to not get in their way. This means you need to do these three things:

- Help them find out what they *want* to do. Is what they are contemplating something they care about? What kind of assets do they have to get underway? What is their next low-cost step?

(Could you introduce them to someone you know?) Your goal here is to help them be creactive.

- Aid them in understanding current reality as best they can. Desire and passion can distort reality, a potential Achilles' heel for people trying to start something new. They can get so caught up in what they want to do that maybe they don't perceive current reality as clearly as they might. ("Why wouldn't the mayor want to fund my idea? It makes all the sense in the world," they tell you. "I can't imagine that raising property taxes is going to be a big deal, given the obvious benefits of what I want to do.")

- Reinforce Creaction when you observe it. For example, point out that they seem excited about the idea (if they are), and that the risk doesn't seem all that high (if it isn't). Reinforcing behavior is the fastest way to embed new thinking. So when you see a friend or a family member taking a really smart, low-cost step, you can applaud and reinforce her behavior. It's probably ten times more powerful than reinforcing her thinking.

These approaches will be really helpful for people in any setting. Let's see how they might play out with family and friends.

## Creaction and family

We love our families and friends. So we say this with all the love and affection possible: using Creaction with either group will be a real challenge, but it is possible.

To illustrate, we have invented Sara Carlton and her family. Sara is pretty typical. She works at Global Diversified Industries (GDI), an international conglomerate based in the United States. She met her husband, Dan, at the company twenty years ago. They have two kids:

Becky, fourteen, and Scott, eleven. Sara is active both in the community (she serves as the parent representative to the school board in Gladstone, Missouri) and in her church.

Dan, who writes speeches for the chairman of GDI, is convinced he has spotted a potentially huge opportunity and has been dreaming for years about starting a company to pursue it. In our story, Dan tells Sara that he is finally decided whether he should leave his well-paying job and strike out on his own.

Companies like GDI have tons of intellectual property (IP), but they neither employ every bit of it, nor have a need to keep it proprietary forever. True, they use some of that IP to establish a competitive advantage in the marketplace, but after they do, it often lies fallow.

Dan has explained on numerous occasions to both Sara and their friends:

> It doesn't have to be that way. Toyota sold its first-generation hybrid technology to the Detroit car companies, once it started working on the fourth generation of the Prius. That's exactly the sort of thing companies could do with their intellectual property. After they used whatever portion they are going to employ to increase their market share, profits, or whatever, they could turn that IP into business review articles, op-eds, white papers, books, videos and software, etc., that could be sold or used, in essence, as high-end marketing materials like op-eds and thought leadership pieces. And I would be the perfect person to help those firms figure out what they have that could be of interest to others and then I could develop them.

In Dan's initial vision, he would quit GDI and start this new company. Sara, thanks to her understanding of Entrepreneurial Thought and Action principles in general, and Creaction in particular, has convinced him that:

- Thinking about this any further will get him nowhere. The only way to discover if the idea will work is to take a small step toward finding out and seeing what happens.

- Taking a dramatic step, such as quitting his job, isn't necessary. He probably could do a lot of the prep work—finding companies whose IP he could mine; lining up writers, video people, and software developers who could channel the IP—on nights and weekends and during lunch.

Sara has been supportive—"I am glad to see your enthusiasm remains high; have you thought about talking to Bill Tabor over at Galaxy International [a GDI competitor]? He is now the head of all their communication efforts and is probably the entry point over there." But Dan hasn't talked about the idea for a while, so she doesn't have a clue what he is about to say as they sit down at the kitchen table. For the first time in a long time, her husband surprises her. "I am ready to do it," he begins with no preamble.

> I've worked up prototypes of the stuff I could sell, using GDI material. I showed it to the CEO and he was impressed. So if this idea bombs as a freestanding company, I think I can do it internally at the very least. But I have five companies interested. I've lined up a bunch of freelancers and production people, so we are good to go. But to get everything rolling, I need the $25,000 we have put away to help pay for the rec room addition we have planned. I have to pay the freelancers a little bit to get them to start work; I need to set up an LLC, buy the domain name, and pay a Web designer to help me. And I should probably have a cushion, since I am guessing the business will be

cash-flow negative for a while. You know how long it takes big companies to pay their bills. Is it okay with you if I use all that money?

And with that question, you get to a key difference between how Creaction functions in business and how it works among family and friends. There are more dimensions, different emphases, more complexity, and far more nuances outside a commercial setting.

With arm's-length business transactions, the issue of acceptable loss might be about money, time, resources, and opportunity costs. For example, "If we do X and it doesn't work, we will be out $Y and will have blown the opportunity to have done Z (the other alternative we were considering)."

Most of this is pretty transparent and not necessarily emotionally loaded. Money is simply a fungible commodity; it is not something that is being saved for Becky's college education, a new roof, or an emergency. Reputation is often a factor, but it is more often public reputation: "Josh is a great salesman; Josh is a lousy salesman."

---

If you are married, when it comes to acceptable loss, the question to ask is not, "How much am *I* willing to lose?" but, "How much are *we* willing to lose?"

---

When you are dealing with family, there are different and potentially serious costs to your relationships with the people you care about. For one thing, as Dan realizes, if you are in a relationship, there is no such thing as your own acceptable loss. The potential loss affects your partner (and possibly your children as well). Then there is the potential loss of face with your family. How is your spouse going to feel about you if the new venture fails? Will your kids think less of you if you end up spending their college fund on an idea that flames out? In the case of family, the psychosocial dynamic and potential cost are almost always enormously important.

Moreover, in an arm's-length business transaction, failures generally have fewer long-term consequences. The project will succeed or be unsuccessful. The deal will get done or it won't. But it is a rare case in which the decisions are of the bet-the-company variety.

Conversely, the kinds of things you do in a family situation may reverberate for decades. To oversimplify, if you failed to get the Henderson account, it may hold back your career for a while. But if you were the person who repeatedly warned your father-in-law about investing in Google ("Why would anyone want shares of a search engine company?") right before the company went public, and he followed your advice and put his money in an alpaca farm instead, Thanksgiving dinner with your spouse's side of the family may become very, very awkward for years and years.

So the steps you take with family generally appear to be more irrecoverable. (You can move to a new company or city; it's hard to move to a new family.) As a result, the acceptable loss calculation you do is quite different. Not only may the amount of money you are prepared to lose be less (your spouse or partner may be risk averse; you may be more predisposed to play it safe, fearing the reaction of those near and dear to you, should you fail). And things are different when it comes to self-selected stakeholders, as well.

In a straightforward business transaction among people who know each other slightly (or not at all), everyone generally understands the nature of the deal. People bring obvious resources to the table, and it's pretty clear what they expect in return.

But when you are involved with family, those things can often be far less clear, and they are frequently conflicted. Family members may want to support your efforts, but maybe you don't want them to—at least not too much. (Do you really want to be beholden to your in-laws forever for the funding that got you started?)

As a supporter, you may find it very easy to lend emotional support, while at the same time being unable (or unwilling) to exhibit financial support. This can cause complex and complicated feelings for the actor. ("I know my sister has the money I need. Why won't she invest it in my company?")

Just the opposite might be true in another case. ("Sure, my brother lent me the money, but he did it out of guilt. He never really believed in me.") Perhaps even more important, there are often hidden strings—maybe many, many hidden strings—attached. The self-selected crew that you're operating with here is not as neat and tidy as it is in a business setting.

When parents and children are involved, it can become especially complicated. It is hard to imagine your parents *not* being part of your self-selected, committed stakeholder group in some way or another. Even if you aren't counting on them (or don't want them to come along at all), they're going to think of themselves as involved. That's their job. So you are going to have a presence that you can't ignore. And there are a set of expectations that are biologically induced, complicated, and unavoidable. They have perhaps the most profound need to support, educate, and backstop you. You're going to get what *they* think is support whether you want it or not. And they have some real expectations in return, some of which you cannot change.

So, dealing with family is extremely tricky. But in the case of Sara and Dan, things went relatively smoothly. The rec room addition will wait. Dan is going to start his own business.

## Creation and friends

In the best of all worlds, your friends provide the same love, encouragement, and support that your family does. (And often in the real world, they provide those things when your family doesn't.) But because they are emotionally involved with you, all the interpersonal dynamics just described will be in play here, too.

Since we already pointed out the negatives, there is no reason to dwell on them here. Instead, let's talk about how taking smart steps could work effectively with your friends and the social groups you are involved with. Consider, for example, how Sara and her friends were able to create an indoor basketball court in town.

Sara was on the high school basketball team, so it is not surprising that every Wednesday night when the weather was nice, you could find her playing hoops with a bunch of her friends. While playing on someone's backyard court during late spring and summer was fine, the Midwestern fall, winter, and early spring are cold, and there was simply no place for Sara and her friends to play indoors. The local school gyms were constantly in use, and the nearest Y wasn't convenient. As a result, except when there were unexpected warm spells, Sara and her friends didn't play much basketball from November through April.

They wanted to change that. If they followed Prediction, they would have met with the Gladstone parks director and convinced him to draw up a plan and then lobby the town council for both the $1 million it would take to establish a recreation center and the additional $100,000 a year in the municipal budget to cover the cost of staffing and maintaining it. Municipal governments working as they do, and town budgets being as they are, the center might have been ready right around the time that Sara's grandchildren would be working on their behind-the-back dribbles and dunks.

Having seen how Creaction had worked for Dan and her sister (see "Can You Use Creaction as a Dating Guide?"), Sara wondered if it would be effective here as well. She contacted everyone she knew and asked them to reach out to everyone they knew to spread the word that a group of neighborhood women were trying to create an indoor basketball center at little or no cost.

## Can You Use Creaction as a Dating Guide?

Creaction, we discovered to our surprise, also works on an extremely personal level. Consider, for example, romance.

Sara's sister, Cyndi, divorced for two years, has gone the Prediction route when trying to find love these last twenty-four months. She has joined computer matching services, signed up with places that arrange "just lunch" dates, and spent time in the restaurants and bars identified by *Kansas City Magazine* as "the best for singles." When asked to describe the results of all this, she says, "Not great."

Having heard her sister explain how Creaction works, she has an unusual reaction: "It sounds like the perfect dating strategy."

Understanding she could start anywhere within the process, Cyndi began by defining what she wanted: "a man who is fun to be with." Another marriage was not on her immediate agenda. From there, she asked the key questions:

**Who am I?** What traits, tastes, and inclinations do I have? How do they align with the potential guy I am searching for? Having double-checked current reality, she has concluded that there has to be a certain percentage of single guys who want to spend time with a woman who has no immediate expectation of marriage.

**What do I know?** Cyndi believes her education, training, experience, and expertise make her attractive.

**Who do I know?** This question has her excited. She is convinced that by telling everyone in her personal, social, and professional networks that she is going to use Creaction to find dates, her social life will improve. It turns out she is right. The people in her various networks know lots of guys who might fit her criteria, and they are happy to make introductions.

Cyndi continues to use Creaction as she follows up on all the names. She talks to each man by phone (investing just a small amount of time, so it's well within any acceptable loss). If the conversation goes well, she suggests they meet for coffee. If the face-to-face meeting is promising, she decides she is willing to invest more time (a dinner date, perhaps). At each step of the process, she is deciding whether it's worth taking an additional step. It's the quintessential example of Creaction, and as Cyndi told us, "It is working very well for me."

Countless e-mails were exchanged over the next few weeks—and all of them led nowhere. True, the acceptable loss was small, just the time it took to write and read the e-mails, but it was still frustrating. Then a friend of a cousin of one of the women who played occasionally in the Wednesday night games suggested that Sara call her older brother: "He works for Mizzou Manufacturing, you know, the company that is downsizing? His job is to sell off all the unwanted assets. They have an old warehouse about a mile away from you that I think could work as some sort of gym."

She was right, and we will condense the next nine months into two paragraphs.

The manufacturing executive said he would be happy to donate the building, just to keep the company from paying taxes on it. One of the basketball regulars, an attorney, created Hoopstar Dreams, a nonprofit organization, to accept the gift. The women then lobbied local businesses for the loan of machinery and donation of supplies—the donors got to display permanent ads courtside—to turn the inside of the warehouse into a small recreation center. Seemingly everyone even vaguely related to the women spent the next thirty-six Saturdays doing the actual labor, under the supervision of a general contractor (the husband of one of the basketball regulars).

When the building was done, the board of the nonprofit, comprising Sara and her friends, agreed to lease the building to the Gladstone recreation department for $1 a year in exchange for a promise the town would staff the building and pick up all maintenance and insurance costs. (It is far easier to get a town to commit to hiring a couple of people and pay for operating expenses than it is to get them to lay out $1 million in a single shot, and local officials had an additional incentive to do the deal. They had been searching for a place for a town-sponsored day-care program, and the building, which Sara and her friends would use only at night and on weekends, was perfect.)

These days, just about every Wednesday night, no matter what the weather, you can find Sara playing basketball at the Hoopstar Dreams Recreation Center.

## Just Start:
## An Exercise for Explaining Creaction to Others

People tell us that sometimes they get stuck when they try to explain the logic of Creaction to someone who has never been introduced to it before. This might help serve as a template.

"Fred, I would like to be able to create or accomplish X. Doing so would be really meaningful to me for these reasons: A, B, and C. This is why I want to do it. I can't predict right now if this is going to work. But in the situation I'm in, action is really much smarter than doing nothing. So I want to act.

"It's reasonable to act now because the cost is low. And maybe you've got some ideas about me lowering it further. And it's not just me by myself. I have these other people around who want to help me.

"So, that's what I want to do. And I think you could play a big part by doing Z."

# Takeaways

1. **Yes, Entrepreneurial Thought and Action works with family and friends, but . . .** The "but," of course, is the emotional component. Not planning for it is just silly when you are dealing with family and friends. It needs to be a huge consideration.

2. **The acceptable loss calculation is substantially different with family and friends.** This point follows the last. When you are dealing with people near and dear, you can lose a lot more than money if something goes wrong. Plan accordingly.

3. **Remember to play both roles.** In dealing with family and friends, you can apply Creaction when you are the one trying to bring something into being (Sara wanted to have a place to play basketball in winter) and when you are supporting someone else (Sara enabled Dan's new venture).

# 10

# How Creaction Can Make a Better World

We aren't engaging in hyperbole with that headline. Entrepreneurs can use Creaction to solve what seem to be unsolvable problems—everything from the health-care crisis to social ills.

Broadly speaking, there are two ways Creaction and the broader concept of Entrepreneurial Thought and Action can make a better world: creating jobs and solving big problems.

SAY WHAT YOU WILL about politicians, they understand that it is always about the economy and creating jobs. They should probably add Creaction to their tool kits.

As we saw in chapter 8, large, publicly traded firms have added no new jobs—when you net layoffs and retirements—over the last twenty-five years. Large organizations have innovated, and it is probably true that the positive effects of those efforts have been the one thing that has kept job creation from being considerably more negative. But when you net everything, entrepreneurial ventures (stand-alone and within existing organizations) are the only ones creating jobs and allowing people to join—and remain—in the middle class. Yes, a significant number of start-ups fail, losing as many jobs as they create. But some start-ups become high-impact growth enterprises that hire a lot of people. That's why they account for all the job growth. There is no known method that predicts which of the many start-ups will become the "gazelles," or high-impact growth enterprises, nor how to help a particular venture become more gazelle-like at its inception. The only way to have more of these firms is to have more start-ups.

In terms of making a better world, the benefits are obvious, both psychological and material, to the actor (the person who ends up with the new job), his or her family, and to the communities of which they are a part. Successful entrepreneurship will renew decaying cities, lower crime rates, and breathe life into local institutions, such as churches and other community groups. Over the decades, entrepreneurship has enabled the world's poor to advance, and when combined with micro-finance solutions, becomes an important advance in the war on poverty that in turn usually leads to political stability. One of the major sources of political unrest and the rise of global terrorism is the total lack of jobs for young men.

But Creaction is useful in an individual's life in more ways than just creating new businesses. Creaction gives you more influence everywhere in your life. You are a driver as you head down the highway, not a passenger. Being behind the wheel always gives you more control and more options. Increased control over one's environment is one pathway to greater self-confidence and personal fulfillment. While the accomplishment of big goals is certainly a wonderful thing, for many, maybe even all of us, our mood, motivation, creativity, and general happiness all increase as we see ourselves making progress on the things that matter to us—a perfect description of Creaction at work.

## Solving intractable problems: The tyranny of top down

Many policy makers and experts believe that effective large-scale change needs to be driven from the top down and must be rooted in deep planning ("big problems require big solutions"). Yet experience shows that is probably not the case. These huge problems involve so many fundamental constituencies that trying to organize them to move forward together collapses under the weight of political ideology, infighting, and competing personal agendas.

If we look at three of the grand problems of our time—health care, energy, and education—all of them have fundamentally resisted top-down intervention, and all of them now are starting to yield to local or community-based, bottom-up experimentation. Yes, we have large numbers of people who are thinking deeply about these issues. We don't want that to stop, but we need to understand that that deep thought needs to merge with evidence, evidence which is produced by smart action, that helps us figure out where to go.

Massive change can evolve from the bottom up. The "Arab Spring" we saw in the Middle East in early 2011 is one of the more powerful indications of the ability of people to self-organize entrepreneurially to obtain what they want.

One major advantage of taking small, smart steps is that it helps to overcome what we have come to think of as "the tyranny of the optimal right answer."

We desperately want certain things to be better, and we turn to the planners, policy makers, and experts to help us. The problem is, of course, these experts don't agree. While some tell you something can be done, others say it can't. (Or "it will have horrific side effects," or "someone else has tried something similar and it did not work," or . . .)

The problem here is not that the future is unpredictable. Each side is near-certain about its prediction. It's just that these predictions utterly contradict each other. One expert is certain about something, and another is certain about exactly the opposite. The result is an image of the future that is potentially predictable to some degree, but effectively unknowable because of the lack of any common ground Net, we end up at an impasse and nothing happens.

The way to break this inaction is with small, smart, creactive steps that are limited by acceptable loss. You don't know what is going to happen, and the only way you're going to find out is to take a step and see where you are and figure out what the next step is after that.

Creaction argues for taking a number of new, small, smart steps—a pilot project here, a different way of doing things over there—to see what happens. Positive outcomes can be built upon the experiments that show promise.

In a world where nobody really knows (or one that you must treat that way), you want to generate as many solutions as possible. Taking such smart steps is an essential key to making the impossible possible. Smart action in the face of the unknown is better than arrested (or no) progress due to more debate.

Many who are intellectually oriented will say, "Oh no, when you are facing a complicated situation, it is better to think it through because until you understand it, you're likely to take a disastrous step." But small steps are not disastrous, even if they are wrong. Big, high-impact ideas have their place. However, there is no evidence that *only* through big ideas do we resolve the issues.

For example, in 1972, President Jimmy Carter called for wholesale changes in the behavior of Americans to fundamentally reduce our dependence on foreign oil. Mileage requirements for cars went up dramatically, and certain conservation efforts became mandatory. Today, our dependence our foreign oil is higher than it was then.

Yet, at the same time, we have seen that the steps both individuals and organizations have taken on their own, in their communities, or with their employers to reduce their carbon footprint have spread on a large scale. These smart actions show much more promise for being able to address these issues than our ability to move big policy initiatives through government.

## The tyranny of the scalability requirement

When we point out how individuals—not government—seem to be making the most progress in decreasing energy consumption, we hear, "Well, that's marvelous! But, it can't scale."

---

The idea behind "scalability" is ultimately that you need one big solution. But why would that be true? Maybe lots of small, local ideas would be just as good.

---

Our society has blithely decided that any public policy idea is subject to the requirement that it be scalable to 300 million (or 7 billion) people, but there is no reason that every idea has to be a big one. You don't want to edit yourself out of entrepreneurial activity because it's not going to be a revolutionary page-one story in the *New York Times*.

Besides, the question of scalability is often a matter of placing the proverbial cart before the horse. An individual or corporation, or for that matter, government, may think they have a big idea, but none are the ultimate decider of whether it is, in fact, good. Only the market (commercial or political) can decide. Said another way, we don't grow our ideas and products; our customers (or our citizens) do.

Since it is often hard, if even possible at all, to predict what our customers will do (and even more so what future customers will do) maybe a better strategy for coming up with the big idea is to start with as many promising ones as possible. And clearly Creaction can help there.

If a million people are acting in a million small ways, the question of scalability is potentially irrelevant, as long as the system improves. It doesn't have to be optimal action, at first, just progress.

On June 6, 1966, at the University of Cape Town, South Africa, Robert F. Kennedy (then a U.S. senator from New York) said:

> Few will have the greatness to bend history itself, but each of us can work to change the small portion of events, and in the total of all those acts will be written the history of this generation. It is from numerous diverse acts of courage and belief that human history is shaped. Each time a man stands for an ideal, or acts to improve the lot of others, or strikes out against injustice, he sends forth a tiny ripple of hope, and crossing each other from a million different centers of energy and daring, those ripples build a current that can sweep down the mightiest of walls of oppression and resistance.

A lot of us don't want to necessarily tackle global warming or change the world; we want to improve our neighborhoods, our streets. We can. Each of us can become "positive deviants," and out of these small wins will come results that other people will observe and some of them will build off what we have created. Take the education crisis in the United States. We actually know there are two things that will make a difference, teachers and principals. These two factors are more influential than buildings, government funding, and everything else. So what can you as an individual do? Instead of trying to influence education on a national level—getting stumped by the magnitude of the problem in the process—you can instead concentrate on getting one more good teacher and/or principal hired. Over time, these small successes will enroll others and help fix the big issue by enrolling even more people. And, for the reason we talk about next, the time it takes for that enrollment to happen is probably going to decrease.

As you know, we live in an increasingly open-source, social world. Ideas can come from any place and go to any place, largely independent of language or culture. In the predominantly physical world of the 1900s, it was time consuming to get a message from place to place. Obviously, the Internet changed that and has also allowed like-minded people to self-organize online.

Anything that works is communicated more broadly and more rapidly than ever before in history. Good ideas made public will find audiences of interested parties to implement locally. All this interconnectiveness radically changes the ability of a single, good idea to have massive influence. We can now network little steps into big leaps.

## A little help from our institutions

Entrepreneurial Thought and Action and, more particularly, Creaction really can improve our lives. But that change for the better will occur far faster if the largest institutions in society participate. And, as we said, they are starting to. Let's take a look at what they are doing and what we would like them to do.

### Government

As we write, one of the top priorities at the federal level is making the United States more entrepreneurial. Entrepreneurialism is seen as the best way to grow the economy. Our government has taken its responsibility seriously and is actively trying to foster the creation of more new businesses. This is a good thing.

As we have seen, government can encourage Creaction by funding small projects to attack big problems like health-care costs. One reason health care is so expensive is because of malpractice suits and the attendant costs of litigation. A pilot project in New York City, funded by the federal government, is currently experimenting with ways to settle lawsuits sooner and at lower costs. Will it work? No one knows. But it is an experiment worth making.

But this book is about Creaction and how it can be applied in daily life. Can government cause entrepreneurial thought? The short answer is not really. And it shouldn't. That's not its role. This isn't bad news. Entrepreneurialism has flourished since the dawn of civilization. Our society is built on millennia of entrepreneurial acts. Entrepreneurial thinking is built into our genes. We will think and act entrepreneurially with or without government. If government has a primary role, it is to prevent interference.

Government can promote the opportunity for individuals to both think and act to address issues in their community, and then scale these ideas into more fundamental solutions, rather than waiting for large policy-oriented solutions to come from the top. Solutions are more lasting and more positive if rooted in the behavior of individuals rather than the prescriptions of government.

And there may be one other role government can play: helping educators.

## Schools

Our educational institutions' job is to teach thinking. The Creaction we are advocating is easy to teach, because people already know it. They only need to practice it more. That can happen if it is seen as a legitimate complement to the Prediction reasoning that pervades our educational system.

We're not talking about more courses or substituting courses. We simply argue for adding a deliberate, conscious "action component" to what is already being taught. We want students to recognize, when faced with a problem where Prediction may not yield a satisfying answer, that it is a logically legitimate time to try Creaction.

Schools currently emphasize teaching people stuff at the expense of teaching them how to act. The educational process of preparing people for an assumed exclusively predictive world is fundamentally getting in the way of building a generation of people for whom smart action will be a habit as well, an *additional* part of their repertoire. So we essentially make the argument for conscious experimentation in schools to build, or at least keep people from losing, their action skills alongside their cognitive skills, legitimizing the way of thinking and then getting people to practice it.

For example, the Babson College strategy revolves around a robust cocurricular experience that is focused on enabling people to live entrepreneurially alongside learning entrepreneurship—living math alongside learning math, living science alongside learning science. We believe that such forms of experiential learning are going to lead to a generation of far more effective actors.

You already see this taking place. Many cooperative programs in engineering schools aim to get students out into the world to practice what they learn. The key is to introduce it as early as possible. Think back to our discussion of bilingualism in chapter 9. Children effortlessly learn additional languages and move back and forth between them. As you get older, it becomes far more difficult. It is the same when you are trying to teach ways of thinking as well. Adding Creaction could be exciting and could reinvigorate tired teachers and school systems, lifting all disciplines and uniting them to provide our society with citizens capable of twenty-first-century jobs, because they are capable of twenty-first-century thinking.

## Business

What about our businesses? Will they foster entrepreneurial thought? We've discussed how Creaction is counter to how large organizations reason. Yet, experimentation is increasing. Companies that are not meeting their growth targets are looking for new alternatives. Witness the current interest in open innovation, design thinking, and the like. There is every reason to believe that creactive efforts are ongoing, even though they may be covert in many cases. Business will be validating the value of the creactive logic.

Business also offers a great propagation mechanism—second only to individual entrepreneurial effort. Anything that promotes better business results and competitive advantage—as Creaction does—can quickly find acceptance in companies around the globe. Total quality or six-sigma, reengineering, customer relationship management, and economic profit are all ideas that started locally, proved themselves, and spread.

## Social ventures and religious institutions

Social ventures are another matter. Social entrepreneurial ventures are sprouting up because of deep needs. The principles in this book fit perfectly.

The directors of these ventures should take notice and stop requiring the overuse of formal planning, which everyone knows is foolish when facing the unknown. Directors need to release their social entrepreneurs from the shackles of exclusively using Prediction and instead learn how to better support their creactive efforts.

You might find it odd that we include religious with social ventures. It's exceedingly rare that religion is entrepreneurial in its orthodoxy and things often do not go smoothly when it tries. (Martin Luther comes immediately to mind.) On the other hand, we've seen a lot of evidence of Creaction in the leadership that our religious institutions play in human rights and social justice. (Martin Luther King Jr. and the civil rights movement, for example.) And we have seen how it is being used in the founding of new nondenominational churches, synagogues, and mosques. The missionary work of various churches all are creactive efforts in the face of the unknown.

## Coming full circle

So, our government can provide incentives and can remove barriers to Creaction.

Businesses can experiment, prove Creaction's value, and compete.

Social entrepreneurs can build new agencies and establish communities of like-minded people.

But most important, we—as parents, teachers, and students—can reclaim our heritage as creators.

All we need is to desire it, act quickly with what we have at hand, take small steps, bring our friends along, and build on what we find.

Just start.

# *Epilogue*
# Responses to Some Challenging Comments and Questions We Receive

PEOPLE ARE NATURALLY SKEPTICAL ABOUT CREAC-
TION, and rightfully so. If you are going to become an advocate for
Creaction, and we hope you are, you can expect pushback. Here is how
we respond to the comments and questions we get.

### 1. This whole thing sounds too simple.

We know you didn't mean that as a compliment, but we would like
to say thank you anyway. Making this simple and easy to understand
was our intent. At its most basic, Creaction, a method that we believe
can augment the way you think now, is something that we all did before we were introduced to more formal ways of reasoning.

As an infant, toddler, and preschooler, everything you confronted
for the first time was an unknown. Because it was, you tried certain
things. You cried. You tried to walk. You put your finger in a light

socket. And as a result of your actions, certain things happened. Some good (walking). Some bad (that shocking light socket). But that is how you dealt with what, at the time, was an unpredictable universe for you. You took small steps to learn about it.

This way of approaching life has become unfamiliar to us over time, because it has been replaced by the Prediction reasoning used to explain reading, writing, and arithmetic, and just about everything else. But, our natural way of learning—the approach we had as children—has remained within us. We just want to help bring it out.

**2. What the heck do you guys know about life in the real world? Why should I believe that this is anything other than just another egghead theory?**

You're right about our backgrounds (although each of us has had substantial profit-and-loss responsibility throughout our careers). But the last thing we hope you do is take this on faith. Belief will get you nowhere; only action will. Either this makes enough common sense for you to try it or it doesn't. Don't take our word for it. Take a small, smart step and see if it feels right to you. If it does, take another.

**3. Your whole argument can be reduced to "ready, aim, fire," can't it? Isn't that stupid on its face?**

As we've said, the summary really is: aim, fire. There's not a lot of getting ready. At its heart, we are saying that when you are in a situation where you don't know what is going to happen next, and the cost of acting is low, then fire with what you have at hand or can assemble quickly.

As for "stupid," you won't know if it's stupid for you until you try it. Until then, all you have is the thought that this may be stupid. That thought sure won't take you anywhere. (By the way, this approach has been proven by smart, successful serial entrepreneurs. They don't think it's stupid. That's what intrigued us in the first place.)

**4. Who has time for taking steps down a road that may lead nowhere? I have a finite amount of time, resources, and energy, and I simply can't afford to waste them.**

Agreed. But you really have only three options when faced with the unknown: (1) You can think forever and conclude the situation is hopeless or the problem is too big, so you do nothing. (2) You can do all that thinking, and when you are absolutely, positively, sure, you act . . . only to find out that (a) you may not have been right, or (b) while you were doing all that thinking, someone beat you to the solution or the solution changed. (3) You can do enough thinking to take a smart step toward a solution, one that won't cost you a lot if you are wrong (leaving you enough resources to try again).

**5. I will grant you that maybe this could work for people thinking about starting a small business, but I need $500 million for the biotech company I want to start. How is this going to help me?**

It's probably not, at least not beyond the early phases of your project, which, by the way, is where biotech entrepreneurs and others who need a lot of money use it. Clearly, you can use all the principles of acceptable loss to help you determine if you are truly committed to starting your manufacturing facility, biotech lab, or whatever the venture is that will consume a lot of capital. And once you get your money, you will use Creaction in your product development to some degree.

But at some point, you are going to need to attract serious money. And that will mean finding serious investors, investors who are going to rely on—and will want you to rely on—Prediction. That's perfectly fine. Remember what we have said. Creaction—and acceptable loss is part of Creaction—isn't designed to replace Prediction. There are still going to be many places—such as raising huge amounts of capital—where Prediction, with its emphasis on future cash flows and return on investment, is going to be the way to go. This is one of those places, so predict away.

**6. This is never going to work in the big company where I work.**

You may be right. But as veterans of working in and with big companies, we know this: they will commit to anything that will help them make more money legally. They are not going to reject it out of hand if there is a promise that it will make them more successful. (If they do, the idea has been presented badly.)

**7. Have you met our mayor? Town council? School board? Clergy? What do you mean, it can work in all aspects of my life?**

Until you act, all you have is your thoughts. If you think it can't work and you don't act, you will be left with the thought that it can't work, and that will be a self-fulfilling prophecy.

Our whole argument is that you need to act to create what you want. Once you have acted, you have evidence. The evidence may confirm that this approach may not work with your town council—you really won't be able to overcome the politics that will get in the way—and maybe it won't work with your clergy. But we have seen it work with governments and religious organizations. The bottom line: until you act, you will never know for sure.

**8. Maybe all this could work in business, but you don't know my mother-in-law, wacky sister, or offbeat friends. How can you possibly think this will work with families and friends?**

You're right. It probably won't work with in-laws. (That was a joke, if our in-laws are reading this. [If they aren't, it wasn't.])

But although the dynamics are different with family and friends— the acceptable loss concept is far more important, for example—we have seen the concepts work and even help people get dates.

**9. If this is such a good idea, how come it is not being taught in schools?**

Our question exactly. Our schools are now training people who are going to be in the workforce in the year 2065. Who can predict what they will need to know? Since they are going into the vast unknown, they should be armed with as many potentially helpful tools as possible, and clearly Creaction can be one of them. Our schools really are the place to teach thinking. And the thinking we are advocating here is easy to teach, because people already know it. They only need to practice more. Our suggestion: Don't add any new classes. Just fold Creaction activities into what you are teaching now, beginning in prekindergarten and continuing through the postgraduate level.

**10. How can you possibly believe this can change the world? The problems we face are too intense and immense.**

They are. And Entrepreneurial Thought and Action in general and Creaction in particular are hardly the whole solution. But they are part, the neglected and insufficiently applied part. After all, entrepreneurs have made some absolutely wonderful contributions to humankind through the literally millions of things they have brought into being.

The beauty of Entrepreneurial Thought and Action is that it creates a defined logic or reasoning around this thing called Creaction, which otherwise looks like a black box. It allows people to make Creaction explicit and apply it in any area of their lives. It just becomes ordinary.

That takes us full circle, of course. People are bound to read what we have to say and think, "But I knew that." That's our hope.

*Takeaway:*

## The One-Minute Creaction Seminar . . . the Book in Seventy-Eight Words

1. **Know what you want.**

2. **Take a smart step toward that desire as quickly as you can,** that is, act with the means at hand; stay within your acceptable loss and bring others along with you if it makes sense.

3. **Make reality your friend.** Accept what is and build off what you find.

4. **Repeat** steps two and three until you accomplish your goal or until you decide it is not possible, or you decide you'd rather do something else.

# Further Reading

From the dedication, you can see how important the research of Saras Sarasvathy has been to us. Her book, *Effectuation: Elements of Entrepreneurial Experience,* describes the thought and action processes of serial entrepreneurs. To learn more, visit www.effectuation.org, where she and her colleagues run an active Web site.

On first exposure, we found her ideas exciting and original and we wanted to explore them more deeply (desire). In February 2009, we created a course, Action Trumps Everything (www.actiontrumpseverything.com) and invited our friends and colleagues (got started with the means at hand). The only resources required were our time and a little money to rent the classroom (within our acceptable loss), and thus we were able to keep the tuition pretty low. Each session incorporated the feedback and experiences of the participants (entrepreneurs, aspiring entrepreneurs, social entrepreneurs, families, friends, supporters, bosses of entrepreneurs—ages sixteen to seventy-plus) (built off what we found) who participated in a process of codeveloping much of the framework you have read in the previous pages. These folks invited their friends and colleagues to the next sessions (they brought others along).

In the course of these seminars, we ended up discovering a number of additional ideas we added to our original notions. We made up the word Creaction in part to point to these additions and to distinguish it from Sarasvathy's effectuation. In late 2010, we published *Action Trumps Everything* (Black Ink Press) based upon our learning from the course sessions and from additional explorations of multiple literatures, some of which are cited later.

The most significant of the outside ideas we added is the importance of *desire* as a complement and counterpoint to uncertainty. A source on this subject is William Irvine's *On Desire.*

Closely linked to desire are the ideas of discovering and creating opportunities. There is an enormous amount written about these subjects. One good source on the creative process is *The Path of Least Resistance* by Robert Fritz. On an entirely different tack is *Old Masters and Young Geniuses* by David Galenson.

Enrollment is the third element not found in effectuation. Here we built off the pioneering work of Innovation Associates in organizational learning as described by

Peter Senge in *The Fifth Discipline* and in many human potential workshops of the last forty years. Lewis Hyde's, *The Gift,* carries great descriptions of the spirit behind enrollment.

In parallel with our efforts, the Babson faculty (Danna Greenberg, Kate McKone-Sweet, and H. James Wilson) has written *The New Entrepreneurial Leader*, which lays out a comprehensive framework for reinventing management education in order to help develop leaders who can and will shape social and economic opportunity.

Peter Sims has written a book we enjoyed, *Little Bets,* which covers some of the same subject matter we have addressed in this volume. His "Further Readings and Resources" chapter is a great source for further exploration.

The vast majority of the ideas presented in this book have withstood academic scrutiny and practical verification independently of each other—in some cases, over many decades—but so far, they have not been integrated in the fashion we have presented except in our courses. While there is no existing research history on the entire model, people with lifetimes of entrepreneurial experience have provided significant verification based upon their life experiences. In keeping with the book's premise, we believe that's good enough for now.

# Acknowledgments

This book is essentially a report of what we have learned from the hundreds of people who have attended the Action Trumps Everything workshop. We owe a special thanks to these alumni and friends: Dick Balzer, Paul Bauer, Les Charm, Mike Chmura, Mary Jo Cook, Eliot Daley, Wayne Delker, Pete Dolan, Diane Fulman, Carol Hacker, Kerry Hamilton, Miriam Hawley, Sherry Immediato, Cheryl Kiser, Martin Krag, Kurt Malkoff, Doug Milliken, Amy Rosen, Julia Ross, Johann Sadock, Richard Voos, Joel Yanowitz, Carl Youngman, and Ken Zolot.

And we would especially like to acknowledge for their untold hours of work helping to develop and express the ideas in their present form: Shahid Ansari, Scott Aronow, Chuck Conn, Heidi Sparkes Guber, Heidi Neck, Stever Robbins, and Steve Tritman.

We are enormously grateful for the support, enthusiasm, and contributions given to us by our wives: Carolyn Kiefer, Phyllis Schlesinger, and Alison Davis Brown; and our children Peter Brown, Shannon Brown, Becca Schlesinger Ferat, Megan Kiefer, Adam Payne, Jarl Payne, Katie Schlesinger, Emily Schlesinger, Nick Viscomi, and Sam Viscomi, who have contributed to the manuscript and the course, and perhaps most importantly, contributed through their lives as case studies of Entrepreneurial Thought in Action.

Finally, for helping us turn a manuscript into a finished book, we would like to thank Ann Crews, Kristen Palson, Rebecca Saraceno, Stephani Finks, Melinda Merino, Jen Waring, and the rest of the staff at Harvard Business Review Press.

# Index

# About the Authors

**Leonard A. Schlesinger**, president of Babson College, came to the school from Limited Brands where he was vice chairman and chief operating officer. His academic career includes twenty years at Harvard Business School.

Len is the author or coauthor of nine other books including *The Value Profit Chain* and *The Real Heroes of Business . . . and Not a CEO Among Them.* He earned his doctorate at Harvard Business School, an MBA from Columbia University and his A.B. from Brown University.

**Charles F. Kiefer** is president of Innovation Associates, the firm that helped pioneer the body of concepts and methods now called organizational learning.

Charlie helps global companies leverage the human side of their enterprise primarily by working with executives and their teams to improve the quality of their thought. He attended the Massachusetts Institute of Technology where he received degrees in physics and management.

A long-time contributor to the *New York Times,* **Paul B. Brown** is a former writer and editor for *BusinessWeek, Financial World, Forbes,* and *Inc.* He is the author (or coauthor) of numerous bestsellers, including *Customers for Life.*

Paul is a contributing editor to both the MIT *Sloan Management Review* and *The Conference Board Review.* He earned his A.B. and J.D. at Rutgers University.